The Non-Stop Discussion Workbook

Second Edition

Problems for Intermediate and Advanced Students of English

George Rooks

English for Foreign Students Program
University of California at Davis

HEINLE & HEINLE PUBLISHERS
A Division of Wadsworth, Inc.
Boston, Massachusetts 02116

Director: Laurie E. Likoff
Production Coordinator: Cindy Funkhouser
Production: R. David Newcomer Associates
Cover Design: Katherine von Urban
Illustrator: Karl Nicholason
Compositor: TypeLink, Inc.
Printer and Binder: Malloy Lithographing Inc.

The Non-Stop Discussion Workbook, Second Edition

ISBN-13: 978-0-8384-2938-9
ISBN-10: 0-8384-2938-6
Library of Congress Cataloging-in-Publication Data

Rooks, George.
   The non-stop discussion workbook.

    1. English language—Textbooks for foreign speakers.
2. Discussion. I. Title.
PE1128.R64   1988   428.3′4   88-5182

22 23 24 25 07

63-24917

Photo credits: Unit 2: Cliff Moore/Taurus Photos; Unit 4: *TV Host Weekly*, copyright 1988 by TV Host Inc.; Units 5, 12: National Education Association/Joe DiDio; Unit 6: Eric Kroll/Taurus Photos; Unit 7: Richard Wood/Taurus Photos; Unit 10: American Stock Exchange; Units 11, 15: Japan Air Lines; Unit 18: Laimute Druskis/Taurus Photos; Unit 23: Manschenfreund/Taurus Photos; Unit 26: courtesy of Levi Strauss & Co.; Unit 27: United Nations; Unit 28: NASA.

Contents

Introduction

This second edition of *The Non-Stop Discussion Workbook* is for intermediate and advanced students of English. It continues to offer a practical and imaginative approach to the discussion class.

New to This Edition

- The units have been restructured into five headings: Read, Consider, Decide and Write, Discuss, Extend.

- The completely new "Extend" section contains numerous, provocative questions and activities designed to enable the students to transcend the realm of values clarification.

- The units have been reordered, and two new units have been added.

- A number of units have been changed internally to facilitate discussion, and two units have been deleted.

- Potentially difficult vocabulary words are marginally glossed, and a glossary of these same terms appears at the end of the text.

- There is a new mix of photographs and drawings that accompanies each unit and helps to provoke discussion.

One of the main problems with discussion classes is that the teacher talks too much and the students talk too little. Perhaps this is because the students find the subject of the discussion uninteresting; perhaps it is because the silent members of the group do not want to talk. For whatever reason, the discussion period often turns into a harrowing question-and-answer session in which little "discussion" takes place. The purpose of this workbook is to generate discussions in which the students do *almost all* the talking.

To accomplish this, the students are given a stimulating problem they must solve and a straightforward method of solving it. Most of the problems pose serious and challenging dilemmas, ranging from life-and-death situations to planning a new city. The problems deal with a wide variety of subjects, designed to appeal to as many students as possible. Each problem is presented on the page through a combination of photographs, drawings, and text. The photographs and drawings set the scene. The text is divided into five sections: Read, Consider, Decide and Write, Discuss, Extend. The "Read" section introduces the problem; the "Consider" section sets out the factors to be weighed in the problem-solving process; the "Decide and Write" section gives guidelines for reaching a decision and asks that students write down their ideas before the discussion takes place. The "Discuss" section directs students to orally consider the problem. Finally, the "Extend" section encourages the class as a whole to consider issues raised by the problem. In addition, the students are often asked to extend themselves beyond discussion into other modes, such as composition.

There are many possible methods for solving each problem, and teachers are encouraged to be flexible. Most methods, however, have four basic stages: First, the teacher introduces the problem to the whole class; second, the students are given a short time to consider the problem and write down their solutions; third, the class is divided into small discussion groups, each of which discusses, analyzes, and eventually solves the problem (as a group); fourth, there is a follow-up stage in which the groups compare their solutions.

These problems work best when the discussion groups have from four to six students. For example, a class of 15 students could be divided into three groups of five students each. It is best to have as few people who speak the same language in each discussion group as possible. Small discussion groups work best because: (1) students often feel more willing to talk among themselves in a small group than with a teacher in a large group; (2) the small discussion group will put shy students more at ease; (3) the fewer people in the discussion group, the more English each group member must speak.

It is important that the teacher feel free to be flexible. One problem a day will tire the most energetic students; so will a method of presentation that never varies. To overcome these difficulties, the teacher might assign a problem as homework so that students will have more time to think about the problem and master difficult vocabulary words contained in it. Or the students can be given 10 or 15 minutes to work out the problem individually, after which the teacher can lead a group discussion of the problem. Because flexibility is so important, the following use of class time is given merely as a suggestion, as a starting point to build upon and change.

Suggested Use of Class Time

(based on a 50-minute class)

Day One

A. Presentation of Problem (15–20 minutes)

The teacher introduces the problem by briefly discussing the photograph and/or drawings. The teacher then reads the entire problem aloud while the students follow along silently. The teacher makes sure that the students completely understand the situation and the considerations. In addition, the teacher should briefly go over new vocabulary words. The teacher then gives the students at least 10 minutes to reread the problem and write down their decisions. Finally, the class is divided into small discussion groups.

B. Discussion (30–35 minutes)

The small discussion groups work through the problem and arrive at an agreed solution. While the problem is being discussed, the teacher walks through the class answering whatever questions arise, listening in on discussions, and resolving any difficulties. As a show of confidence in the students' ability to conduct discussions independent of the teacher, the teacher might occasionally leave the room and occupy him/herself with other matters. These things can be done while the students work on the problem.

Day Two

C. Comparing Solutions (20–25 minutes)

This can be done in different ways. One method is to make a grid on the board and have a member from each group fill in the group's choices. Here is an example of a grid for the problem "Ordering a Baby."

	Group 1	Group 2	Group 3
Hair Color			
Eye Color			
Height			
Weight			
Future IQ			
Personality			
Profession			

After the students have filled in their groups' choices, the teacher acts as a moderator—pointing out significant similarities or differences and asking groups to give the reasons for their particular choices. (The students will not have enough time to comment on all their choices.)

Another method is to compare solutions verbally; however, this will not generate as much discussion because the different groups cannot see the other groups' selections.

D. Extending (25–30 minutes)

This is a step away from values clarification and towards an in-depth analysis of some of the issues raised by the problem. One way to approach this part is as a class—that is, the class as a whole, not in small discussion groups, will respond to the questions posed. A number of units contain activities that may extend the class to a third day.

George Rooks
University of California, Davis

Acknowledgments

I would like to begin this new edition of *The Non-Stop Discussion Workbook* by thanking all of those teachers worldwide who have successfully used the first edition of the text in their classes since its publication in 1980. Particularly pleasing have been the warm letters from the English teachers in such diverse places as Somalia, Costa Rica, Italy, the People's Republic of China, Indonesia, Burkina Faso, Venezuela, Oman, and Tahiti, to name but a few. My sincere thanks are also given, of course, to all my colleagues both here at the University of California and at other institutions in the United States who have received the book so well.

And what of the Korean school of engineering that uses the unit on town planning? Or the Warsaw sociology department that includes the unit on what is representative in the U.S. in its course on American culture? Or the Japanese corporation in Tokyo that uses problems such as that in Unit 1 in its seminars on relationships with developing countries? I can only say that the use of this text outside the English classroom has been especially interesting and gratifying to see.

I would be remiss not to restate here, as in the first edition, my enduring thanks to all my students present and past who have made such valuable contributions to the text.

Again, I dedicate this book to my parents, Miriam and George, from whom I learned the art of intelligent discussion. I dedicate this particular edition to my wife, Hila, for all of her invaluable suggestions and support.

The Non-Stop
Discussion Workbook

What Gets the Money?

Read

You are the **Budget** Department of the new South American country of Amazonas, which has just been created from parts of southeastern Colombia and northwestern Brazil. Located **in the heart of** the Amazon jungle, Amazonas (pop.: 100,000; area: 125,000 sq. mi.) has abundant, undeveloped natural resources (iron, gold, diamonds, oil); however, most of the **indigenous** population experiences the negative effects of primitive living conditions.

  The Prime Minister of Amazonas has just directed your department to decide how to spend this year's $2 million budget. For which of the following items on the list do you recommend **funding**, and what percentage of the budget should each item you select receive?

budget: financial plan

in the heart of: in the center of

indigenous: native

funding: money

PROGRAM 1: AGRICULTURE

Consider

Most Amazonians suffer from **malnutrition**, especially the children. In fact, over 70% of the children currently receive less than one-fourth of the calories necessary for a healthy life. Agricultural conditions are poor because most of the country is **dense** rain forest.

malnutrition: poor diet

dense: heavy

% of budget: _____ Reasons: _____

PROGRAM 2: TRANSPORTATION
Consider

tributaries: small rivers carrying water to a large river

Boat travel on the Amazon River and its **tributaries** is the main form of transportation in the country. There are few roads and no airports or railroads.

% of budget: _____ Reasons: _____

PROGRAM 3: POLICE AND NATIONAL GUARD
Consider

lured: attracted

Amazonas has already begun to experience increasing crime from the influx of adventurers **lured** by the prospect of sudden riches. Moreover, the government fears that if Amazonas' natural resources are developed, Amazonas' large neighbors might not honor its independence.

% of budget: _____ Reasons: _____

PROGRAM 4: EDUCATION
Consider

scattered: spread

Capana, the capital of Amazonas, has two high schools. There are also a few missionary (religious) schools **scattered** throughout the country. However, there are no universities, and over 90% of the country is illiterate.

% of budget: _____ Reasons: _____

PROGRAM 5: DEVELOP UTILITIES
Consider

Over 95% of the country still does not have electricity despite the tremendous potential for hydroelectric power. No people outside the capital have refrigerators, stoves, or even electric lights.

% of budget: _____ Reasons: _____

PROGRAM 6: DEVELOP NATURAL RESOURCES

Consider

Iron, gold, diamonds, oil: the money gained from developing these resources could make Amazonas a rich country benefitting all of its citizens. As yet, however, there are no mines or oil wells.

% of budget: _____   Reasons: _____

PROGRAM 7: SOCIAL SERVICES

Consider

There is only one doctor for every 5,000 citizens, and only one small clinic in the capital of Capana. There are no hospitals. The infant mortality rate is extremely high, and the average life expectancy in Amazonas is low (men: 39; women: 42).

% of budget: _____   Reasons: _____

PROGRAM 8: COMMUNICATIONS

Consider

Amazonians have telephone service only in the capital. There is a primitive postal service. Telegraph and television are nonexistent.

% of budget: _____   Reasons: _____

PROGRAM 9: PUBLIC RELATIONS

Consider

Amazonas needs people and foreign investment. The Prime Minister feels that some means should be found to attract new settlers and investors from other countries to help develop Amazonas.

% of budget: _____   Reasons: _____

PROGRAM 10: PROTECTION OF INDIGENOUS POPULATION

Consider

impending: coming

The government strongly feels that the native people of Amazonas (particularly Indians) must be protected from the **impending** problems of development.

% of budget: _____ Reasons: _____

administrative manpower: managers

PROGRAM 11: TECHNOLOGICAL EXPERTS AND ADMINISTRATIVE MANPOWER

Consider

Amazonas simply does not have enough qualified people at present to run existing programs efficiently or to design new ones.

% of budget: _____ Reasons: _____

Discuss

Verbally compare your decisions with those of the classmates in your discussion group. Explain and defend your opinions. Listen carefully to your classmates' opinions, but do not be afraid to disagree with those opinions. Try to reach a group concensus on the best solution to the problem. One person in the group should write down the group's decision.

Extend

1. There are many terms used for countries such as Amazonas: non-industrialized, underdeveloped, developing, Third World, technologically new. Which term do you prefer?

2. What is the main problem that faces most developing countries?

3. Do developed countries have a responsibility to help developing countries? If yes, why and how?

4. What are some reasons that developed countries might want to **hinder** Third World countries from developing?

hinder: block, slow down

5. List three positive and three negative effects of industrial development. Give examples.

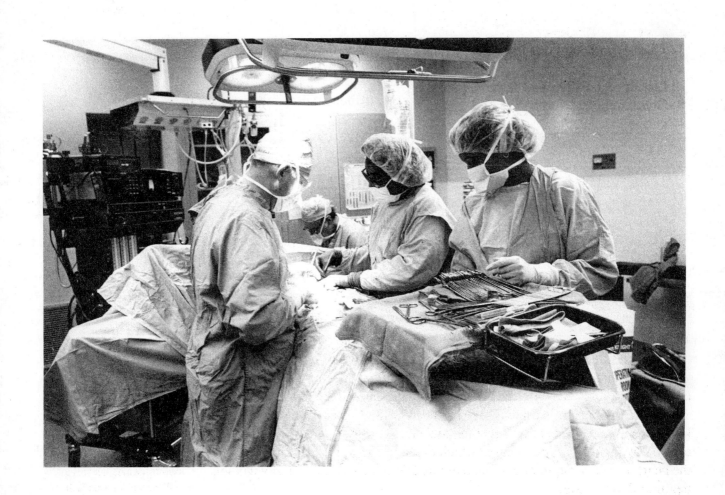

Who Gets
the Heart?

Read

You are members of the heart transplant surgery **team** at a university hospital in Washington, D.C. At the moment, you have seven patients who desperately need a transplant if they are to have any chance of living. All seven patients are classified as ''critically ill,'' and could die at any time.

   You have just received news that the heart of a 16-year-old boy who was killed in an auto accident has become available for transplantation. Speed is extremely important as you decide which of the following patients is to receive the heart: not only might one of the patients die, but the **donor** heart will soon begin to **deteriorate.**

team: group

donor heart: heart that will be put in a patient

deteriorate: become worse

Consider

1. The age and sex of the donor has no relationship to the age and sex of the **recipient.** In other words, the heart of the 16-year-old would work well in a 50-year-old woman. Size, however, might be a consideration in the case of the infant.

recipient: receiver

2. Rank the option/patients in order of preference: 1 = first to receive, 8 = last to receive.

Decide and Write

Patients

renowned: famous

inspiration: source of encouragement

deteriorating: worsening

1. Amegneza Edorh, female, age 57. Mrs. Edorh, a **renowned** poet and novelist from Nigeria, received the 1987 Nobel Prize for literature. An **inspiration** throughout the developing world because of her anti-colonialist writings, Mrs. Edorh has been confined to bed for the past five months with steadily **deteriorating** health.
(Married: four children between the ages of 30 and 37)

Reasons she should receive the heart: _____

Reasons she should not receive the heart: _____

Ranking of heart transplant team: _____

dramatically: rapidly

2. Soohan Kim, male, age 12. Soohan, a junior high school student from South Korea, was born with a congenital heart defect. Doctors wanted to wait until he was a teenager to replace his heart, but his condition has worsened **dramatically.** He is being kept alive on a heart-lung machine.

Reasons he should receive the heart: _____

Reasons he should not receive the heart: _____

Ranking of heart transplant team: _____

3. Alicia Fagan, female, age 27. Ms. Fagan's heart problems, though recent, seem to have a genetic basis inasmuch as her twin sister (patient 4) is similarly affected. Although Ms. Fagan is a promising Ph.D. student in biochemistry at Georgetown University, her failing heart and kidneys have caused her to drop out of school temporarily. (Unmarried)

Reasons she should receive the heart: _____

Reasons she should not receive the heart: _____

Ranking of heart transplant team: _____

4. Galia Feinstein, female, age 27. Mrs. Feinstein is Ms. Fagan's twin sister. Mrs. Feinstein, who holds a Master's degree from Harvard University in computer science, currently operates a computer business with her husband. (One daughter, age 4.) Mrs. Feinstein's condition differs from that of her sister in that her kidneys have not been affected.

Reasons she should receive the heart: _____

Reasons she should not receive the heart: _____

Ranking of heart transplant team: _____

5. Leonid Gromykovitch, male, age 34. Mr. Gromykovitch works for the U.S. government as a researcher for the Central Intelligence Agency. Born in the Soviet Union, Mr. Gromykovitch is considered the Agency's foremost Kremlinologist (Soviet expert). Like patient 2, Mr. Gromykovitch is being kept alive on a heart-lung machine. Unmarried (his wife died in an automobile accident), he has three children (ages 6, 3, 2).

Reasons he should receive the heart: _____

Reasons he should not receive the heart: _____

Ranking of heart transplant team: _____

6. Martha Rosales, female, age 23. Mrs. Rosales' heart problems originated from a **bout** she had with scarlet fever while growing up in the slums of New York. Unemployed and on **welfare,** Mrs. Rosales raised money for her operation through the contributions of those in her neighborhood. Never married, she has four children (ages 8, 6, 5, 1).

bout: battle
welfare: government money for poor people

Reasons she should receive the heart: _____

Reasons she should not receive the heart: _____

Ranking of heart transplant team: _____

7. Peter Jacobsen, male, age 42. Mr. Jacobsen's family has a history of heart disease (his father died from a heart attack at age 39). Considered the leading scientist in the world in the area of bacteriological diseases, Mr. Jacobsen has already had one heart transplant operation. Since his body rejected that heart (three weeks ago), Mr. Jacobsen has been kept alive by an artificial heart. (Never married, no children)

   Reasons he should receive the heart: _____

   Reasons he should not receive the heart: _____

   Ranking of heart transplant team: _____

8. None of the above. Save the heart for someone else.

   Ranking of heart transplant team: _____

Discuss

Verbally compare your decisions with those of the classmates in your discussion group. Explain and defend your opinions. Listen carefully to your classmates' opinions, but do not be afraid to disagree with those opinions. Try to reach a group concensus on the best solution to the problem. One person in the group should write down the group's decision.

Extend

1. Do you think that only doctors should decide who receives transplants? Are there any other people who should help make such decisions?

2. What do you think about cross-species transplants—such as putting a baboon heart in a person?

3. How do you think you would feel if you received the heart of another person? How would it feel to have another person's heart in your chest?

4. When you die would you be willing to **donate** your **organs** to a person who needs them? Explain.

   donate: give

   organs: body parts such as eyes, heart

5. When do you think a person is dead and therefore capable of giving his organs to another: when his brain has no more activity, or when his heart stops beating?

Ordering a Baby!

Read

The year is 2250. Your family group has decided to have two new children. Since the 20th century, the method of having children has **radically** changed. Instead of the old way, now each family group decides on the **characteristics** it wants its child to have and orders the child from the local factory. Fill out the following application forms for your new baby girl and baby boy.

radically: completely
characteristics: features (for example, height, weight)

Consider

1. Racial characteristics (skin color, etc.) are not a primary consideration, since they will be determined primarily by the characteristics of the family group (the government allows little **variation** in this matter).

   variation: flexibility

2. In terms of IQ, 100–120 is considered ''normal''; 140 or above is considered ''genius''; around 250 is the highest ever calculated for anyone.

3. _____ : indicates a different choice of your own.

Decide and Write

FUTURO BABY FACTORY: ORDER FORM

Names of group applying:

Date:

Characteristics (please circle your choice):

1. *Sex:* male, female

2. *Color of eyes:* red, yellow (blonde), green, brown, black, turquoise, blue, tan, white, _____ .

3. A. *Color of hair:* red, yellow (blonde), green, brown, black, turquoise, blue, tan, white, _____ .

   B. *Type of hair:* straight, curly, wavy, _____ .

4. *Future height* (feet/inches): Shortest _____ Tallest _____

5. *Future weight* (pounds): Heaviest _____ Lightest _____

6. *Future IQ* (100–200): Lowest _____ Highest _____

ambidextrous: capable of using both hands equally well

7. *Coordination:* right-handed, left-handed, **ambidextrous.**

8. *Personality* (unlimited choices):

friendly	shy	quiet	talkative
unemotional	emotional	optimistic	pessimistic
passive	aggressive	idealistic	**realistic**

passive: not active, but acted upon

realistic: practical

_____	_____	_____	_____

9. *Areas to **excel** in* (choose three): sports; music; art; dance; science; humanities (language, economics, social sciences); hand work (plumbing, etc.); _____ ; _____ ; _____ .

excel: do extremely well

10. *Future profession possibilities* (choose five): poet, musician, artist, writer, plumber, electrician, carpenter, research scientist, professor, doctor, lawyer, **real estate agent,** police officer, firefighter, salesperson, forest ranger, sportsman, pilot, military person, secretary, computer programmer, technician, religious person, chef (cook), _____ , _____ , _____ .

real estate agent: seller of land and houses

11. Please explain in 50 words or less why we should process your order (why you want a baby).

Decide and Write

FUTURO BABY FACTORY: ORDER FORM

Names of group applying:

Date:

Characteristics (please circle your choice):

1. *Sex:* male, female

2. *Color of eyes:* red, yellow (blonde), green, brown, black, turquoise, blue, tan, white, _____ .

3. A. *Color of hair:* red, yellow (blonde), green, brown, black, turquoise, blue, tan, white, _____ .

   B. *Type of hair:* straight, curly, wavy, _____ .

4. *Future height* (feet/inches): Shortest _____ Tallest _____

5. *Future weight* (pounds): Heaviest _____ Lightest _____

6. *Future IQ* (100–200): Lowest _____ Highest _____

7. *Coordination:* right-handed, left-handed, abidextrous.

8. *Personality* (unlimited choices):

friendly	shy	quiet	talkative
unemotional	emotional	optimistic	pessimistic
passive	aggressive	idealistic	realistic
_____	_____	_____	_____

9. *Areas to excel in* (choose three): sports; music; art; dance; science; humanities (language, economics, social sciences); hand work (plumbing, etc.); _____ ; _____ ; _____ .

10. *Future profession possibilities* (choose five): poet, musician, artist, writer, plumber, electrician, carpenter, research scientist, professor, doctor, lawyer, real estate agent, police officer, firefighter, salesperson, forest ranger, sportsman, pilot, military person, secretary, computer programmer, technician, religious person, chef (cook), _____ , _____ , _____ .

11. Please explain in 50 words or less why we should process your order

    (why you want a baby).

Discuss

Verbally compare your decisions with those of the classmates in your discussion group. Explain and defend your opinions. Listen carefully to your classmates' opinions, but do not be afraid to disagree with those opinions. Try to reach a group concensus on the best solution to the problem. One person in the group should write down the group's decision.

Extend

1. In many areas of the world, it seems that most parents prefer that their first child be a boy. Why might this be so?

2. What is your opinion about artificial insemination?

3. With the many different forms of artificial conception that are now scientifically possible, the prospect of baby factories has moved even closer. Do you think they will ever become a reality? Explain.

4. Write a composition about your parents' expectations of you. What kind of person do/did they want you to be? Have you tried to fulfill their expectations of you? How successful have you been in satisfying their expectations?

Service	7:00	7:30	8:00	8:30	9:00	9:30	10:00	10:30	11:00
5	Three's Company	Family Ties	Boys Will Be Boys	Women In Prison	Adventures Of Beans Baxter	Mr. President	News	Sports Extra	Taxi
9	It's A Living	Mama's Family	Benny Hill	NBA Basketball: New York Knicks at Chicago Bulls					News
11	Cheers	Tales From The Darkside	*Movie* ★★ **"Curse Of The Pink Panther"** (1983, Comedy) Ted Wass, David Niven.					INN News	**"Panther Strikes Again"**
17	Webster	Mama's Family	Star Search		Lifestyles Of The Rich And Famous		To Be Announced	Profile	Discover
29	Star Trek: The Next Generation		Boys Will Be Boys	Women In Prison	Adventures Of Beans Baxter	Mr. President	News	Taxi	Benny Hill
38 56	Lifestyles Of The Rich And Famous		Boys Will Be Boys	Women In Prison	Adventures Of Beans Baxter	Mr. President	Friday The 13th: The Series		Tales From The Darkside
39	People's Business	DeGrassi Junior High	Mystery!		Lawrence Welk Show		Alfred I. DuPont-Columbia Awards In Broadcast Journalism		
44	Air Power	Inside Washington	Lawrence Welk Show		Nature		South American Journey		People's Business
69	News	CNN News	*Movie* ★★★½ **"Come Back, Little Sheba"** (1953, Drama) Shirley Booth, Burt Lancaster.				Crook & Chase	Music City U.S.A.	INN News
AE	World Of Survival	Victory At Sea	World War I	Vietnam	Living Dangerously		Pulaski: The TV Detective		Special Screening
ESP	College Basketball: Pittsburgh at Boston College				College Basketball: Louisville at Memphis State				SportsCenter
LIF	The Sound Of Murder				Lime Street		Sneak Previews	Sneak Previews	Lady Blue
NIC	Star Trek	Inspector Gadget	Laugh-In	Mister Ed	My Three Sons	Donna Reed	I Spy		Mad Movies
TBS	World Championship Wrestling Cont'd		*Movie* ★★ **"Two-Minute Warning"** (1976, Suspense) Charlton Heston, John Cassavetes.						
TNN	Country Kitchen	This Week In Country Music	Ole Opry Live Backstage	Grand Ole Opry Live	USO Celebrity Tour: Wayne Newton		Country Kitchen	Countryclips	
USA	New Mike Hammer		Alfred Hitchcock Presents	Ray Bradbury Theater	Alfred Hitchcock Hour		Hope For A Drug-Free America		**"Terror Of Tiny Town"**
DIS	*Movie* ★★ **"Run, Cougar, Run"** (1972) Stuart Whitman, Alfonso Arau.		Olympic Greats		16 Days Of Glory		Lake Wobegon Comes To Disney		
HBO	*Movie* ★★ **"Howard Duck"** (1986) Lea Thompson. Cont'd		*Movie* ★★ **"No Mercy"** (1986, Drama) Richard Gere, Kim Basinger.				An All-Star Salute To The Improv Hosted By Robert Klein		**"Karate Kid Part II"**
MAX	*Movie* Cont'd		*Movie* ★★★ **"The Fly"** (1986, Horror) Jeff Goldblum, Geena Davis.				*Movie* ★ **"Born American"** (1986) Mike Norris, Steve Durham.		
PLA			Everything Goes	Playboy's Candid Camera	Priv. Moments	Private Party Jokes	Paris Nights I	Electric Blue: Caribbean Love Cruise	
PRI	*Movie* ★★★ **"Alfie"** (1966) Michael Caine. Cont'd		*Movie* ★★ **"Six Weeks"** (1982, Drama) Dudley Moore, Mary Tyler Moore.				*Movie* ★★★ **"Indiana Jones And The Temple Of Doom"**		
SHO	*Movie* ★★★½ **"Radio Days"** (1987) Mia Farrow. Cont'd		*Movie* ★★½ **"Compromising Positions"** (1985, Comedy) Susan Sarandon, Raul Julia.				A Dynamite Evening With Jimmie Walker & Friends		**"Of Nuke 'Em High"**
TMC	*Movie* ★★★ **"Cocoon"** (1985, Fantasy) Don Ameche, Wilford Brimley.				*Movie* ★½ **"Assassination"** (1987) Charles Bronson, Jill Ireland.			*Movie* ★ **"Murphy's Law"** (1986) Charles Bronson.	
ABC	ABC News / or Local Programming* Cont'd		Dolly		Ohara		Spenser: For Hire		News / or Local Programming*
CBS	CBS News / or Local Programming* Cont'd		High Mountain Rangers		Houston Knights		West 57th		News / or Local Programming*
NBC	NBC News / or Local Programming* Cont'd		Facts Of Life	227	Golden Girls	Amen	J.J. Starbuck		News / or Local Programming*

Plan the Perfect TV Schedule

Read

Your country only has one TV network, ABS, and unfortunately it is terrible. Everybody in the country has expressed **discontent** with the present schedule of programs. At long last, the National Communications Board has decided to act. Your group has been **appointed** to plan a new schedule that will be more **appealing** to the people. In short, your job is to devise the perfect TV schedule.

discontent: unhappiness

appointed: chosen
appealing: likeable

Consider

1. You can fill in the blanks in the schedule with nine types of programs:
   A. Religious programs
   B. News programs (local and international newscasts, **documentaries**)
   C. Movies
   D. Cultural programs (plays, operas, ballet, historical programs)
   E. **Cartoons**
   F. Sports events
   G. Educational programs
   H. Entertainment programs (dramas, comedies, talk shows, game shows)
   I. Your choice.

documentaries: news stories

cartoons: animated children's programs

2. You must specify the exact type of news, cultural, and entertainment programs you want.

3. Programs can be as short as 30 minutes but no longer than one hour and 30 minutes.

Decide and Write

I. The Present Schedule

A. Weekday

1:00 PM	News (local)	6:30	Educational
1:30	News (local)	7:00	Educational
2:00	Movies	7:30	Educational
2:30	Movies	8:00	Educational
3:00	Movies	8:30	Educational
3:30	Movies	9:00	Religious
4:00	Cultural (history)	9:30	Religious
4:30	Cultural (history)	10:00	News (documentaries)
5:00	Entertainment (game)	10:30	News (documentaries)
5:30	News (local)	11:00	Sports
6:00	News (local)	11:30 PM	News (international)

Five problems with weekday schedule

1. _____

2. _____

3. _____

4. _____

5. _____

B. Weekend

1:00 PM	Religious	6:30	Cartoons
1:30	Religious	7:00	Cultural
2:00	Sports	7:30	Cultural
2:30	Sports	8:00	Religious
3:00	Sports	8:30	Religious
3:30	Sports	9:00	News (local)
4:00	Entertainment (comedy)	9:30	News (international)
4:30	Entertainment (comedy)	10:00	Movies
5:00	Entertainment (comedy)	10:30	Movies
5:30	Cartoons	11:00	Movies
6:00	Cartoons	11:30 PM	Movies

Five problems with weekend schedule

1. _____

2. _____

3. _____

4. _____

5. _____

II. The New Schedule

A. The New Weekday Schedule

1:00 PM	_____	6:30	_____
1:30	_____	7:00	_____
2:00	_____	7:30	_____
2:30	_____	8:00	_____
3:00	_____	8:30	_____
3:30	_____	9:00	_____
4:00	_____	9:30	_____
4:30	_____	10:00	_____
5:00	_____	10:30	_____
5:30	_____	11:00	_____
6:00	_____	11:30 PM	_____

B. The New Weekend Schedule

1:00 PM	_____	2:00	_____
1:30	_____	2:30	_____

3:00	_____	7:30	_____
3:30	_____	8:00	_____
4:00	_____	8:30	_____
4:30	_____	9:00	_____
5:00	_____	9:30	_____
5:30	_____	10:00	_____
6:00	_____	10:30	_____
6:30	_____	11:00	_____
7:00	_____	11:30 PM	_____

C. To get your schedule off to a good start select the following:

1. Five movies to appear in the first week:

   a. _____

   b. _____

   c. _____

   d. _____

   e. _____

2. Five comedies, dramas, or educational programs to appear regularly:

   a. _____

   b. _____

   c. _____

   d. _____

   e. _____

D. Five sporting events to appear in the first year:

1. _____

2. _____

3. _____

4. _____

5. _____

Discuss

Verbally compare your decisions with those of the classmates in your discussion group. Explain and defend your opinions. Listen carefully to your classmates' opinions, but do not be afraid to disagree with those opinions. Try to reach a group concensus on the best solution to the problem. One person in the group should write down the group's decision.

Extend

1. What is your general attitude toward television? Explain whether you feel that it has a positive or negative impact on society.

2. Imagine that you have two children: 5 and 15 years old. As a parent, how would you control the amount of TV seen by them?

3. Do you think that TV should be programmed 24 hours a day? Why or why not?

4. Should TV stations be privately owned or government owned? Why?

5. Obtain your local TV schedule from a newspaper. How does it compare with the one that you made?

6. Take a television survey. With a classmate, form a list of 10 questions about television programming, and ask your questions to three people outside of your class (preferably native English speakers). Report your findings to the class.

Which School Programs Do We Eliminate?

Read

The city in which you live has just passed a law reducing all **property taxes** by one half. As a result, the city's high school will have its budget **drastically** reduced. The principal of the high school has formed a list of the programs that might be eliminated and has stated that the budget must be **cut** by $550,000 or the school will be forced to close. As a member of the local board of education, it is your responsibility to decide which programs to eliminate.

property taxes: taxes on land, buildings

drastically: severely

cut: reduced

Consider

1. The high school at present has 2000 students and is the only high school in your city.

2. Reducing the salaries of the teachers is against the law.

3. Remember, you must eliminate entire programs; the principal believes that this is a better **policy** than reducing the quality of all programs through cuts.

policy: plan

Decide and Write

gain: receive

1. **Special Languages Program** ($40,000 a year): The school maintains a special laboratory that is unlike any other high school language laboratory in the state. In it a student can **gain** instruction in five special languages (Latin, Arabic, Mandarin, Portuguese, Russian). Instruction in French, Spanish, and German is *not* included in this program.

   Decision of committee (include reasons): _____

   _____

2. **Physical Education Program** ($35,000 a year): At present, each student in grades 9–12 is required to have one hour of exercise each day. During this period, the students usually participate in group exercises such as sit-ups, push-ups, and jogging.

   Decision of committee (include reasons): _____

   _____

extracurricular: outside the classroom

chorus: singing group

debate: verbal argument to decide the best answer to a question

3. **Extracurricular** Activity Program ($95,000 a year): This program provides facilities, equipment, and travel funds for the following sports teams: basketball, football, baseball, soccer, and swimming. Travel funds and administrative money are also provided for the band, school **chorus**, **debate** team, and the Chemistry & Mathematics Club.

   Decision of committee (include reasons): _____

   _____

4. **Reduce the basic curriculum** ($85,000 a year): Specifically,
   A. Require three years of English instead of four.
   B. Require three years of math instead of four.
   C. Eliminate all courses in journalism, economics, philosophy.

   Decision of committee (include reasons): _____

   _____

5. **School bus program** ($65,000 a year): About 15% of the students live outside the city in which the high school is located. Another 10% have parents who work or do not own a car. Thus, the school operates a bus service for about 25% of its students.

Decision of committee (include reasons): _____

_____

6. **School lunch program** ($75,000 a year): The school attempts to provide an inexpensive, **nutritious** hot lunch to those students desiring one. In the past approximately 1100 students were fed each day. The program was started when it was discovered that students performed better in class and were absent less frequently when they received the lunch.

nutritious: healthful

Decision of committee (include reasons): _____

_____

7. **Reduce the number of teachers at the school** ($150,000 a year): One reason for the school's apparent success has been the **relatively** low ratio of students to teachers, about 25 to 1. If we **fire** teachers, the ratio will be about 30 to 1 (70 teachers in all).

relatively: comparatively
fire: throw out of a job

Decision of committee (include reasons): _____

_____

8. **Eliminate one day from the school week** ($100,000 a year): At present each student attends 35 hours of school a week. Cut the number to 28 hours a week, either by having the students attend less time each day or by not having school on Wednesday.

Decision of committee (include reasons): _____

_____

aides: helpers

9. **Eliminate special aides in the classroom** ($64,000 a year): The school employs 32 part-time aides who assist the teachers with students who have special difficulties. For example, there are six ESL aides who work with the students whose first language is not English.

   Decision of committee (include reasons): _____

   _____

10. **Reduce the number of administrative personnel** ($150,000 a year): There are 20 administrative personnel aside from the principal. For example, there is a vice-principal for each grade. In addition, the four school counselors are considered as administrative personnel.

    Decision of committee (include reasons): _____

    _____

Discuss

Verbally compare your decisions with those of the classmates in your discussion group. Explain and defend your opinions. Listen carefully to your classmates' opinions, but do not be afraid to disagree with those opinions. Try to reach a group concensus on the best solution to the problem. One person in the group should write down the group's decision.

Extend

1. What was the best academic class you ever had in high school? Why?

2. Which do you think is more important for high school students: music and art, or sports? Why?

3. Rank the following in order of the amount of salary you think they should receive (1 = highest): _____ lawyers, _____ police officers, _____ teachers, _____ mail deliverers, _____ secretaries, _____ government workers, _____ pilots, _____ nurses, _____ soldiers, _____ doctors. Explain.

4. Should high school be **compulsory** for all people? What about university study? Explain.

compulsory: required

Cast Your Ballot!

cast your ballot: vote

Read

It's the first Tuesday in November in the United States, and a dramatic election campaign is **drawing to a close**. As usual, it has been a long **campaign** of **charges** and countercharges, with millions of dollars spent on each candidate and issue. Now, it's time for you, a resident of New York state, to cast your ballot!

drawing to a close: ending

campaign: process of seeking political office

charges: accusations

Consider

1. All voting in the United States is by secret ballot and is **anonymous**.

2. You will have 15 minutes to mark your ballot secretly before dropping it in the voting box.

3. When all the ballots are in the box, they will be counted by your teacher or by a student committee.

anonymous: without name

Decide and Write

STATE OF NEW YORK
OFFICIAL ELECTION BALLOT

National

For President (Choose one)

☐ Elizabeth McCormick
1. Age: 48
   Job: Economics professor
2. Democrat
3. Less money for military
4. More taxes
5. More money for old/poor
6. For abortion and gun control

☐ John Stevens
1. Age: 69
   Job: Former football player
2. Republican
3. More money for military
4. Less taxes
5. Less money for old/poor
6. Against abortion and gun control

Initiatives

For   *Against*

lottery: gambling game

☐   ☐   1. Change voting age from 18 to 21.
☐   ☐   2. Establish a national **lottery**.
☐   ☐   3. Establish one year of compulsory national service (military or other) for every 18-year-old.

State

For Senator (Choose one)

☐ Ruth Roberts
1. Age: 52
   Job: Congresswoman
2. Democrat
3. Wants peaceful coexistence with USSR
4. Against U.S. aid to rebels in Nicaragua and Afghanistan
5. Strongly pro-Israel
6. For black government in South Africa
7. Against trade restrictions with Japan

☐ Susan Golding
1. Age: 55
   Job: Newspaper reporter
2. Republican
3. Strong anti-USSR

4. For U.S. aid to rebels in Nicaragua and Afghanistan
5. Equal support for Israel/Arabs
6. Supports white government in South Africa
7. For trade restrictions with Japan

Bond Issues and Propositions

For   *Against*

☐   ☐   1. Increase taxes 25% to pay for more schools.
☐   ☐   2. Increase taxes 5% to pay for more prisons and jails.
☐   ☐   3. Increase taxes 3% to pay for more hospitals for
                veterans.   **veterans:** former soldiers
☐   ☐   4. Spend $10 million to advertise tourism and
                improve recreation facilities.
☐   ☐   5. Spend $100 million to give jobs to unemployed
                people.

Local Initiatives

For   *Against*

☐   ☐   1. A law requiring student prayers in school.
☐   ☐   2. A law changing the drinking age from 21 to 18.
☐   ☐   3. A law prohibiting the sale of magazines such as
                Playboy at local stores.
☐   ☐   4. A law permanently limiting the population of your
                town to 50,000 (it is now 45,000).

Discuss

Verbally compare your decisions with those of the classmates in your discussion group. Explain and defend your opinions. Listen carefully to your classmates' opinions, but do not be afraid to disagree with those opinions. Try to reach a group consensus on the best solution to the problem. One person in the group should write down the group's decision.

Extend

1. What issues are most important to Americans (in your opinion)?

2. How do politics in your country differ from politics in the U.S.?

3. What is the role of women in the politics of your country?

4. What are some of the different ways that leaders are chosen in the world? Which do you think is best?

5. In the form of an interview, verbally present the ballot to three Americans, and write down their responses. Report on their responses to your class.

Which Sports Are the Best?

Read

The President of your country is extremely upset! He has just returned from a trip through the country and cannot believe the terrible physical condition of the people. In short, the people of the country are **flabby**, and he wants to do something about it. Specifically, he wants to provide **federal support** to the 12 sports that will most improve the physical condition of the people.

    Since you are a member of the President's Council on Physical Fitness, you must choose the 12 best sports to be funded. Also, he wants you to list the five sports least likely to improve the people's physical condition.

flabby: fat

federal support: government money

Consider

1. The best sports must be equally **accessible** to men and women.

accessible: available

2. At least five of the best sports must be ''minor'' sports as **designated** by the President.

designated: chosen

3. Rank the 12 best sports from most physically demanding (1) to least physically demanding (12).

4. Here is the list you must choose from (*means a minor sport):

archery*	football	karate*	soccer
badminton*	golf	lacrosse*	softball
baseball	gymnastics*	motorcycle racing*	squash*
basketball	handball*	mountain climbing*	swimming
bicycling*	hang gliding*	racquetball*	table tennis*
billiards	hockey (field)*	rowing*	target shooting*
bobsledding*	hockey (ice)*	skating (ice)*	tennis
bowling	horseback riding*	skating (roller)*	volleyball
boxing	jai alai*	skiing (snow)*	weight lifting*
canoeing*	jogging	skiing (water)*	wrestling*

Decide and Write

1. The 12 best sports

Sport 1: _____

Reasons: _____

Sport 2: _____

Reasons: _____

Sport 3: _____

Reasons: _____

Sport 4: _____

Reasons: _____

Sport 5: _____

Reasons: _____

Sport 6: _____

Reasons: _____

Sport 7: _____

Reasons: _____

Sport 8: _____

Reasons: _____

Sport 9: _____

Reasons: _____

Sport 10: _____

Reasons: _____

Sport 11: _____

Reasons: _____

Sport 12: _____

Reasons: _____

2. The five sports least likely to improve physical condition

Sport 1: _____

Reasons: _____

Sport 2: _____

Reasons: _____

Sport 3: _____

Reasons: _____

Sport 4: _____

Reasons: _____

Sport 5: _____

Reasons: _____

3. The three most dangerous sports

Sport 1: _____

Reasons: _____

Sport 2: _____

Reasons: _____

Sport 3: _____

Reasons: _____

Discuss

Verbally compare your decisions with those of the classmates in your discussion group. Explain and defend your opinions. Listen carefully to your classmates' opinions, but do not be afraid to disagree with those opinions. Try to reach a group concensus on the best solution to the problem. One person in the group should write down the group's decision.

Extend

1. Why is soccer the most popular sport in the world? Why not in the U.S.?

2. Which sports do you enjoy participating in more, individual or team? Explain.

3. Which three sports listed above do you think are the most exciting? Explain.

4. Which sport do you think requires the best physical conditioning? Why?

5. On elementary, high school, and university sports teams, should women and men play on the same team? Explain.

Whom Do You Invite to Dinner?

Read

You are having the most remarkable dinner party in history! By **suspending time**, you are able to invite 12 people who are living, or who are dead, to your party. But that is the problem: Which 12 people will you choose?

suspending time: making the past and present the same time

Consider

1. It is unnecessary that the guests be ''important''; you can choose someone who is interesting for other reasons.

2. Perhaps you might want to establish a theme for the evening; one group of guests might like to have fun; another group might like to discuss interesting philosophical questions. Remember that exactly which guests you choose to invite may depend upon the theme. For example, you would not want to invite people who might hate each other to an evening of ''fun and relaxation.''

3. Choose at least two people who are not on the list.

4. Here is a list of possible guests:

Giacomo Casanova	John Lennon	Madonna
Lady Murasaki	Napoleon	Socrates
Moses	Cleopatra	Julius Caesar
Pélé	Golda Meir	Nicolai Lenin
Albert Einstein	Mao Tse-tung	Marco Polo
Mohammed	Maradona	Karl Marx
Stevie Wonder	William Shakespeare	Gandhi
Jesus	Adolf Hitler	Pablo Picasso
Sigmund Freud	Leonardo da Vinci	Ludwig van Beethoven
Confucius	Michelangelo	Johann Sebastian Bach
Marquis de Sade	Sylvester Stallone	Moammar Gaddafi
Aristotle	Mikhail Gorbachev	Lady Diana
Adam	Anwar Sadat	Martina Navratilova
Eve	Buddha	Yassir Arafat
Fidel Castro	Walt Disney	Alexander the Great
Khomeini	Madame Curie	Julio Iglesias

Decide and Write

Dinner guest 1: _____

Reason invited: _____

_____

Dinner guest 2: _____

Reason invited: _____

_____

Dinner guest 3: _____

Reason invited: _____

_____

Dinner guest 4: _____

Reason invited: _____

_____

Dinner guest 5: _____

Reason invited: _____

_____

Dinner guest 6: _____

Reason invited: _____

_____

Dinner guest 7: _____

Reason invited: _____

_____

Dinner guest 8: _____

Reason invited: _____

_____

Dinner guest 9: _____

Reason invited: _____

_____

Dinner guest 10: _____

Reason invited: _____

_____

Dinner guest 11: _____

Reason invited: _____

_____

Dinner guest 12: _____

Reason invited: _____

_____

Discuss

Verbally compare your decisions with those of the classmates in your discussion group. Explain and defend your opinions. Listen carefully to your classmates' opinions, but do not be afraid to disagree with those opinions. Try to reach a group consensus on the best solution to the problem. One person in the group should write down the group's decision.

Extend

1. Women are generally thought to be better conversationalists than men. Why might this be so?

2. Do you prefer people who talk a lot or people who rarely speak? Explain.

3. In your country, what do people enjoy talking about? When and where do such conversations take place?

4. Do you agree that "Conversation is the spice of life"? What does this mean?

5. Imagine that you invited two famous people to your home for dinner last night. Write a two-page dialogue revealing the conversation that took place.

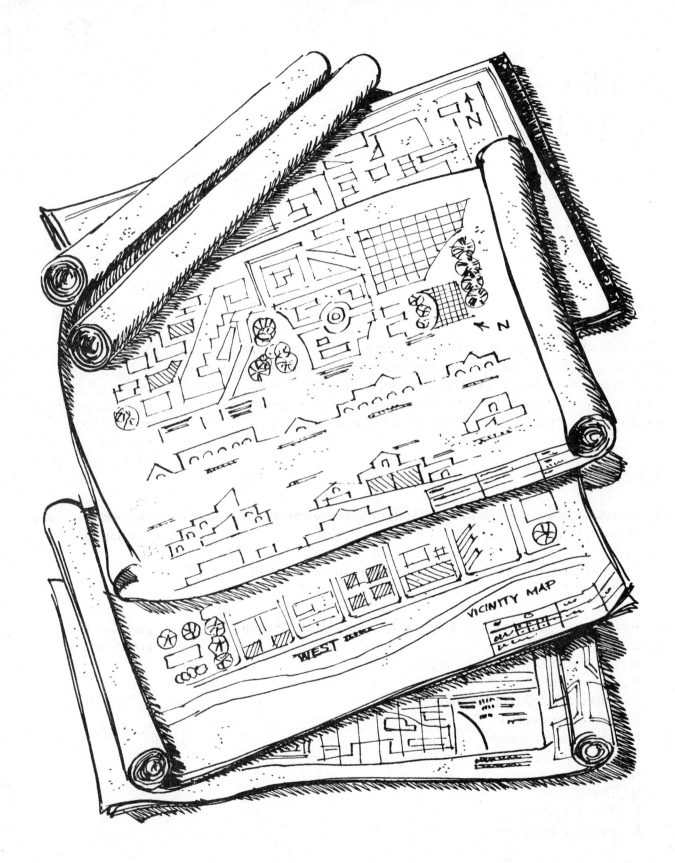

Plan
a Town

Read

One of the most **innovative** architects in your area has just persuaded a group of wealthy people to finance the building of a new town. The location is in the heart of one of the richest agricultural areas in the country. You are a member of a preliminary design committee chosen because of your **creativity** on past **projects**. Your **task** is to design and present a **layout** of the city.

innovative: imaginative

creativity: imagination
projects: jobs
task: objective
layout: plan

Consider

1. Two pages hence you will find a rectangle that **represents** the **boundaries** of the new city. It has an area of three square miles.

   represents: stands for
   boundaries: borders

2. The maximum population of the town at any future time will be 15,000 people.

3. According to the **guidelines** of the county, your city must **initially** have at least:
   A. 1 police station and 1 fire station
   B. 1 sports arena
   C. 2 medical clinics or hospitals
   D. 3 shopping centers
   E. 5 community gardens
   F. 5 community parks
   G. 40 businesses
   H. 1500 houses
   I. 3000 apartments
   J. room for development

   guidelines: laws
   initially: at first

4. For the purposes of filling in areas of the city you will need a ruler or straight edge. Use the blocks on the next page as an indication of size.

5. You may include anything you want.

Discuss

Verbally compare your decisions with those of the classmates in your discussion group. Explain and defend your opinions. Listen carefully to your classmates' opinions, but do not be afraid to disagree with those opinions. Try to reach a group concensus on the best solution to the problem. One person in the group should write down the group's decision.

Extend

1. Most people would rather live in a small town than in a big city. Why is this so? Would you? What are the advantages and disadvantages of each?

2. What can the government of a town do to make life better for its citizens?

3. Imagine that there is one large piece of undeveloped property in the center of a small town. Would you prefer that the land be used for (choose): a park _____, a factory _____, a department store _____, a meeting place for young people _____, tennis and basketball courts _____ . Why?

4. Should the government of a town control each type of building in the town? For example, if a person wants to build a house, should the government approve the plans first? Explain.

detailed: very specific
rationale for: reasons behind

5. Draw a **detailed** map of your native town or city, and explain the **rationale** for its organization.

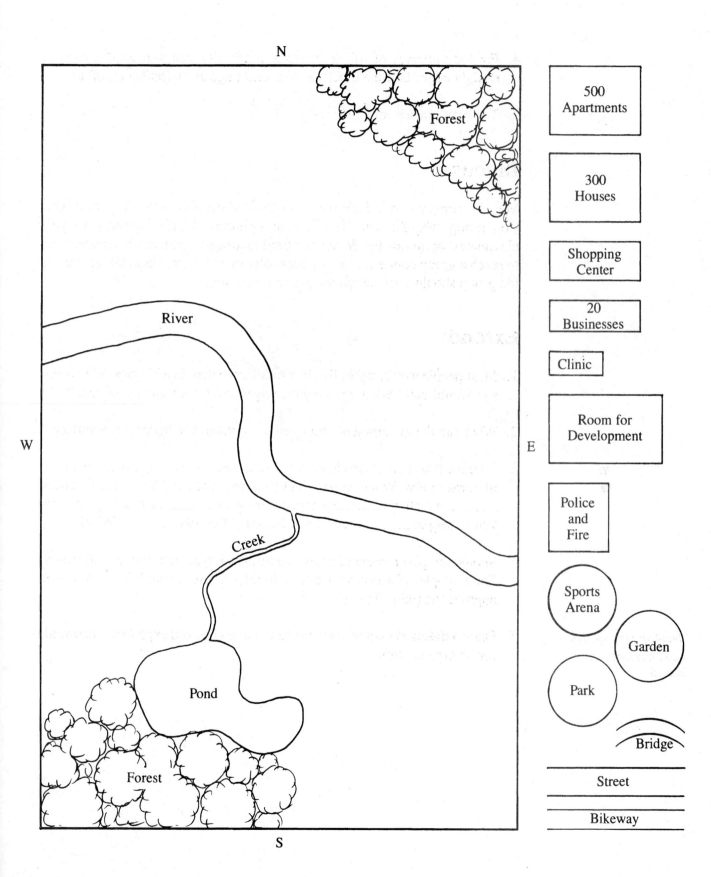

How Do I Invest and Keep My Inheritance?

Read

As you are sitting in the living room of your home, you receive an important telegram **informing** you that your **long-lost** uncle has died and **left** you $2 million. However, your uncle did make two significant **stipulations** in his will. Since he believed very strongly in corporations, he stated that you must invest all the inheritance in corporations. More specifically, he directed that you must invest in at least 15 different companies—and you can put no more than $150,000 in any one company. Second, the **will** states that you have two years to make $500,000 with your investments or the $2 million will be given to your cousin!

informing: telling
long-lost: long-forgotten
left: given
stipulation: restriction

will: legal paper with dead person's wishes

Consider

1. Here is a list of possible corporations for you to invest in:

McDonald's Hamburgers   Toyota Cars
Mercedes-Benz   TransWorld Airlines (TWA)
Aramco Oil   International Business Machines (IBM)
Coca-Cola Co.   International Telephone and Telegraph (ITT)
Gallo Wine Co.   Volkswagen Inc.
Hilton Hotels   Exxon Corp.
General Motors   Columbia Broadcasting System (CBS Television)
Sony   Purina Foods (Animal Foods)
The San Francisco Giants   Revlon (Cosmetics)
Fiat   Proctor and Gamble (Soaps/Personal Products)
Texas Instruments (Computers)   R.J. Reynolds Tobacco Co. (Cigarettes, etc.)
Anaconda Copper Co.   Krupp Armaments (Military weapons)
Dupont Chemical Co.   French National Railroad Corp.
Peugeot (Cars/Bicycles)   Bayern (Medicines and Pharmaceuticals)
General Electric (Appliances)   Xerox Corp.
Greyhound Bus Corp.   Safeway (Grocery Stores)
Bank of America   Pacific Gas and Electric (PG&E)
Minolta Cameras   Metropolitan Life Insurance Corp.
Macy's (Department Store)   Kaiser Aluminum
Levi Strauss (Jeans)   Playboy Enterprises
Swiss National Bank   Harper & Row (Publishing)
Nestle Chocolate

2. You must choose at least one corporation that is not on the list.

Decide and Write

Corporation 1: _____

Amount invested: _____

Reason: _____

Corporation 2: _____

Amount invested: _____

Reason: _____

Corporation 3: _____

Amount invested: _____

Reason: _____

Corporation 4: _____

Amount invested: _____

Reason: _____

Corporation 5: _____

Amount invested: _____

Reason: _____

Corporation 6: _____

Amount invested: _____

Reason: _____

Corporation 7: _____

Amount invested: _____

Reason: _____

Corporation 8: _____

Amount invested: _____

Reason: _____

Corporation 9: _____

Amount invested: _____

Reason: _____

Corporation 10: _____

Amount invested: _____

Reason: _____

Corporation 11: _____

Amount invested: _____

Reason: _____

Corporation 12: _____

Amount invested: _____

Reason: _____

Corporation 13: _____

Amount invested: _____

Reason: _____

Corporation 14: _____

Amount invested: _____

Reason: _____

Corporation 15: _____

Amount invested: _____

Reason: _____

Which five corporations do you think are a bad investment?

1. _____   Reason: _____

2. _____   Reason: _____

3. _____   Reason: _____

4. _____   Reason: _____

5. _____   Reason: _____

Discuss

Verbally compare your decisions with those of the classmates in your discussion group. Explain and defend your opinions. Listen carefully to your classmates' opinions, but do not be afraid to disagree with those opinions. Try to reach a group concensus on the best solution to the problem. One person in the group should write down the group's decision.

Extend

1. Rate the following in terms of what you think is the best investment (1 = best, 6 = worst): _____ gold and silver, _____ oil, _____ savings account in a bank, _____ land, _____ diamonds, _____ stock market (companies).
   Explain.

2. A person once said, ''Don't put all of your eggs in one basket.'' Do you think it is better to invest in many different areas, or in only one or two? Explain.

3. If you had to choose five countries in which to make all of your investments, which five would you choose? Explain.

4. Write a composition entitled ''If I Had $1 million.'' Tell what you would do with the money.

Which Places Do You Recommend?

Read

The **metropolitan** newspaper on which you work is planning a special summer travel **issue**. With the vacation season **approaching**, many readers have written to the paper requesting suggestions for good spots to visit. "Where is a cheap place to vacation?" and "Where is a good place to relax?" are among the most frequently asked questions.

The editor-in-chief has asked your group of travel editors to **compose** several lists of the best places a person can visit and one list of places to avoid. The lists can be based on your personal experience or on what you have read.

metropolitan: large-city
issue: publication
approaching: coming nearer

compose: write

Consider

1. To **insure objectivity**, no member of the group may **nominate** his own country, or a place in his country, for a spot on the lists.

2. An atlas would be helpful to work on the problem.

insure: guarantee
objectivity: fairness
nominate: suggest

Decide and Write

A. The three cheapest places to visit:

    1. _____

    2. _____

    3. _____

B. The three best places to relax:

    1. _____

    2. _____

    3. _____

C. The three countries with the friendliest people:

    1. _____

    2. _____

    3. _____

D. The three most fantastic cities to visit if you have the money:

    1. _____

    2. _____

    3. _____

E. The three most beautiful places to visit:

  1. _____

  2. _____

  3. _____

F. The three worst places to visit:

  1. _____

  2. _____

  3. _____

G. The three most dangerous places to visit:

  1. _____

  2. _____

  3. _____

H. The three safest places to visit:

  1. _____

  2. _____

  3. _____

I. Finally, plan a trip around the world that starts in San Francisco and has you traveling west (maximum 10 stops). Give a reason why you choose each stop.

1. _____   Reason: _____

2. _____   Reason: _____

3. _____   Reason: _____

4. _____   Reason: _____

5. _____   Reason: _____

6. _____   Reason: _____

7. _____   Reason: _____

8. _____   Reason: _____

9. _____   Reason: _____

10. San Francisco   Reason: _____

Discuss

Verbally compare your decisions with those of the classmates in your discussion group. Explain and defend your opinions. Listen carefully to your classmates' opinions, but do not be afraid to disagree with those opinions. Try to reach a group concensus on the best solution to the problem. One person in the group should write down the group's decision.

Extend

1. Rank the following in order of importance when *you* consider a place to vacation (1 = most important, 7 = least important):

    _____ terrorism   _____ friendliness of people

    _____ cost   _____ places to see

    _____ relaxation   _____ language problems

    _____ places to stay

2. Has the increase in terrorist attacks on airplanes made you afraid to fly or not?

3. What are some of the advantages and disadvantages of traveling alone? Of traveling with a large group?

4. Imagine that you are a travel agent trying to attract tourists to your country. Give a 3–5 minute speech about what to see and do there.

Counselors consult about client problems.

How Do I Advise Them?

Read

You are one of a group of social workers at a neighborhood **counseling** center in a run-down section of Newark, New Jersey. Every day several people of different backgrounds stop in to tell you their problems and seek your advice on personal matters. You are paid by the state government to do everything within your power to solve their problems; however, you rarely have to leave your office. Today, five people with **pressing** problems have **dropped in** for advice.

counseling: advising

pressing: urgent
dropped in: come by

Consider

1. You must be extremely careful with your advice; statistics have shown that most people follow the counselor's advice.

2. Be as clear and reasonable as possible.

3. The problems will be told in the speakers' own words.

Decide and Write

Advice Seeker 1: Lisa Sanchez (age 26)

"Cockroaches, rats, a broken toilet, bad wiring, a leaky ceiling: You can't believe what junky condition my apartment is in. This morning, my three-year-old daughter had rat bites all over her legs—I just can't take it anymore! I've complained to the manager and landlord a thousand times. They always promise to fix the place—but they never do anything. Other tenants in the building have the same problems, but no lawyer wants to work for a bunch of poor people. I've looked everywhere for another place for my family to live—there isn't anywhere as cheap. What should I do?"

Advice: _____

_____

_____

_____

Advice Seeker 2: Herbert Jackson (age 49)

shoplifting: stealing from a store

drive us: make us

"I just don't know what to do anymore. My son Jimmy has just been arrested for the third time and is in jail. The first time it wasn't too bad, only **shoplifting**, but this time he broke into a man's store and stole a TV. He's only 17 years old, and I've tried everything. We've taken him to a psychologist, we've talked to him hundreds of times, but nothing seems to work. He's our only child, and it's just about to **drive us** crazy. Please help me. What can I do?"

Advice: _____

_____

_____

_____

Advice Seeker 3: Charlotte Tucker (age 36)

"I really need some help. I know my husband is seeing other women, but I can't do anything about it. I would divorce him tomorrow if I could, but I have four young children to take care of. I never finished high school, so I don't feel I have enough education to get a **decent** job. That's why I have to stay with my husband—for financial support. The more I see him, the more I hate him, but what can I do?"

decent: good

Advice: _____

_____

_____

_____

Advice Seeker 4: Jill Smith (age 14)

"My boyfriend and I have been going together for six months. Yesterday, I found out that I'm pregnant. I told him and thought he'd be happy, but he said he didn't want to see me anymore and that I should get an abortion. I don't really want to get an abortion, but I'm not sure I could support myself and a baby if I quit high school. I haven't told my foster parents yet because I'm so scared; they might send me back to the foster child agency or something. What should I do?"

Advice: _____

_____

_____

_____

Advice Seeker 5: Mary Nathan (age 81)

"Ever since my husband died three years ago, I've been living with my son and his wife and their two children. They live in a three-bedroom apartment three blocks from here. We've always gotten along well before now; they've given me a room and meals, and I've given them some of my **Social Security** check each month. But last night we had a big argument. My daughter-in-law said it was getting too hard to take care of me and they were going to put me in a **nursing home**. My son agreed with her and said he was going to make arrangements for me to leave at the end of the month. What am I going to do? I don't have enough money to get an apartment alone, I don't have any friends, and I'll kill myself before I'll let them take me to a nursing home."

Advice: _____

_____

_____

_____

Social Security: retirement money

nursing home: care facility for old, sick people

Discuss

Verbally compare your decisions with those of the classmates in your discussion group. Explain and defend your opinions. Listen carefully to your classmates' opinions, but do not be afraid to disagree with those opinions. Try to reach a group concensus on the best solution to the problem. One person in the group should write down the group's decision.

Extend

1. Surprisingly, only 3% of Americans over 65 years of age are in nursing homes, and that percentage is decreasing. Why do you think there is such a **misconception** about the number of Americans in nursing homes?

misconception: wrong idea

2. On the other hand, the number of teenage pregnancies in the U.S. is dramatically increasing. Give three possible reasons for this trend.

3. One U.S. state (Minnesota) has passed a law making the parents of a teenager financially responsible for any children the teenager has. Do you think that this is a wise law? Explain.

4. Another alarming social trend in the U.S. is an increasing divorce rate—a trend that the U.S. shares with most other countries. What do you think is behind the worldwide divorce epidemic?

5. Are psychological and social counselors necessary to twentieth century society? What did people who had problems do before the occupations of psychologist and social worker existed?

Plan the Perfect "Core" College Curriculum

core: basic
curriculum: school courses

Read

The **trustees** of your university are very upset by recent studies showing that the average graduate from your school is less **competent** than the average graduate of 50 years ago. As a result, the trustees have insisted that the entire educational approach be changed. Instead of students taking only elective courses, they must take three years (144 units) of "core" courses. Only during their senior year may they take **electives** in their **major**.

According to the trustees, the core courses must be designed to "give the student a broad background in the general humanities and sciences with the result that the student possesses analytical skills and written and verbal ability necessary to be a leader in society."

trustees: directors
competent: capable

electives: non-required courses chosen by a student

major: student's main field of interest

Consider

Each course is four units. You may require a student to take more than four units (or no units) in the following subjects:

anthropology	economics	philosophy
art	engineering	physical education
astronomy	foreign languages	physics
biology	geography	political science
botany	geology	psychology
business administration	history	religion
chemistry	journalism	sociology
composition	linguistics	speech
computers	literature	statistics
dance	mathematics	zoology
drama	music	

THE CORE PLAN (144 units; 12 courses—48 units per year)

I. Freshman Year

   Fall Quarter   *Winter Quarter*   *Spring Quarter*

  1. _____ 1. _____ 1. _____

  2. _____ 2. _____ 2. _____

  3. _____ 3. _____ 3. _____

  4. _____ 4. _____ 4. _____

II. Sophomore Year

   Fall Quarter   *Winter Quarter*   *Spring Quarter*

  1. _____ 1. _____ 1. _____

  2. _____ 2. _____ 2. _____

  3. _____ 3. _____ 3. _____

  4. _____ 4. _____ 4. _____

III. Junior Year

   Fall Quarter   *Winter Quarter*   *Spring Quarter*

  1. _____ 1. _____ 1. _____

  2. _____ 2. _____ 2. _____

  3. _____ 3. _____ 3. _____

  4. _____ 4. _____ 4. _____

Discuss

Verbally compare your decisions with those of the classmates in your discussion group. Explain and defend your opinions. Listen carefully to your classmates' opinions, but do not be afraid to disagree with those opinions. Try to reach a group consensus on the best solution to the problem. One person in the group should write down the group's decision.

Extend

1. When is the best time to choose a major—before university studies? Or at some point during studies (what point)?

2. Is it a good idea for every student to study the same basic subjects before choosing a major?

3. In some countries, such as Japan, there is little relationship between what a student majors in and her **ultimate job**. What do you think of this system?

    ultimate job: job after graduation

4. Rate the following subjects in order of importance to students (1 = most important, 8 = least important):

    _____ psychology   _____ native language   _____ philosophy

    _____ biology   _____ art   _____ mathematics

    _____ foreign languages _____ history

Ask Any Question You Want!

Read

You are being given an extraordinary opportunity to satisfy your curiosity. For many years, you have watched in frustration and anger as people and governments have done stupid things. Also you have watched with wonder and amazement as other people have performed spectacular **feats**, such as a man walking on the moon. Now you can ask any person who has been alive during your lifetime any question you want. For example, you could ask the President of South Africa, ''Why do you continue to have a system of apartheid in your country?''

feats: accomplishments

Consider

1. According to the person who arranged this opportunity, the people who are asked the questions **are obliged to** give you an honest reply.

are obliged to: must

2. You should try to word your question so that a person cannot give a yes/no answer. Moreover, make your questions as direct as possible.

Decide and Write

Person 1: _____

Question: _____

Person 2: _____

Question: _____

Person 3: _____

Question: _____

Person 4: _____

Question: _____

Person 5: _____

Question: _____

Person 6: _____

Question: _____

Person 7: _____

Question: _____

Person 8: _____

Question: _____

Person 9: _____

Question: _____

Person 10: _____

Question: _____

Person 11: _____

Question: _____

Person 12: _____

Question: _____

Discuss

Verbally compare your decisions with those of the classmates in your discussion group. Explain and defend your opinions. Listen carefully to your classmates' opinions, but do not be afraid to disagree with those opinions. Try to reach a group concensus on the best solution to the problem. One person in the group should write down the group's decision.

Extend

1. It is a reporter's job to ask questions. What are some of the difficulties faced by reporters in getting answers?

2. Imagine that you have been sent to interview one of the following people: Adolf Hitler, Josef Stalin, Idi Amin, or Pol Pot? What kind of strategy would you use to interview the person you have chosen?

3. Public figures often complain that they have no privacy. Should their lives be open to *any* question, or are there some things that reporters should *not* ask them about?

4. *Role play:* Assume that one of your classmates is a historical or present personality, and assume that you are a reporter. Make a list of 10 questions to ask him or her. Then reverse the process.

5. Outside of the classroom, talk to five Americans. Ask them: "If you could ask the President of the United States one question, what would it be?" Report your findings to the class.

Raising a Child

Read

As chief researcher in the Department of Health in your city, you have been asked to write a **manual** for parents who are expecting their first child. The Department wants you to assume that the **prospective** parents know very little about raising a child; so you need to be as careful as possible in wording your instructions. You can give guidance based on what you have read or on your personal experience.

manual: handbook of instructions

prospective: expected

Consider

Give reasons for every answer.

Decide and Write

Children (ages birth–12); answer with a short sentence:

1. What type of childbirth should the mother have (natural, under anesthesia)?

   _____

2. Should the father help with the **delivery**?

   _____

delivery: birth

3. If the father does not help with the delivery, how soon after delivery should he see the baby?

_____

nurse: breast-feed   4. Should the mother **nurse** the child or use ''formula'' milk?

_____

5. How long should the baby continue nursing or using ''formula'' milk?

_____

6. How much sleep should the child receive a day?

Birth–2 years old: _____   9–10 years old: _____

3–5 years old: _____   11–12 years old: _____

6–8 years old: _____

7. Should small children (ages 1–3) be put in a playpen or not?

_____

8. A. Approximately how much time should each parent spend with the child?

Female Child

| Ages Birth–6 | Ages 7–12 |

mother: _____   mother: _____

father: _____   father: _____

Male Child

| Ages Birth–6 | Ages 7–12 |

mother: _____   mother: _____

father: _____   father: _____

B. What are activities that the entire family should do together?

_____

9. Should the mother work while the child is at the following ages?

   Birth–2 years old: _____   9–10 years old: _____

   3–5 years old: _____   11–12 years old: _____

   6–8 years old: _____

10. If the mother must work, should the child have a babysitter or go to a day-care center?

   _____

11. At what age is it best to first take a child to a babysitter or day-care center?

   _____

12. A. By what age should a child be "toilet-trained"? _____

   B. How should the child be toilet-trained? _____

   _____

13. A. How should a child be **disciplined** for doing something that is very bad? (Different approaches include: reasoning, spanking, slapping, shouting, **depriving** the child of something he or she likes, sending the child to his or her room, sending the child outside.)

   disciplined: punished

   depriving: taking something away from

   Birth–2 years old: _____   9–10 years old: _____

   3–5 years old: _____   11–12 years old: _____

   6–8 years old: _____

   B. Who (mother, father, both parents) should discipline the child?

   female child: _____   male child: _____

14. How should you teach a child to be self-confident?

   _____

   _____

15. How should you teach a child to be responsible and respect other people?

   _____

   _____

16. What kinds of activities should you encourage the child to participate in when not in school?

   female child: _____

   male child: _____

17. A. At what age (if at all) should a child be told about sex?

   _____

   B. Who should tell the child?

      female child: _____   male child: _____

18. Is there any other important advice you should give the parents?

   _____

   _____   _____

Discuss

Verbally compare your decisions with those of the classmates in your discussion group. Explain and defend your opinions. Listen carefully to your classmates' opinions, but do not be afraid to disagree with those opinions. Try to reach a group concensus on the best solution to the problem. One person in the group should write down the group's decision.

Extend

1. What are the advantages and disadvantages of having children?

2. What factors do you think go into forming a child's personality?

3. Were your parents strict with you? How did they punish you? Will you use the same method with your children?

4. Do you think it is possible that some children "turn out bad" no matter what their parents do?

5. Working parents and divorced parents often say, "It is not the *quantity* of time you spend with your children but the *quality* of time that matters." Do you agree? Explain.

What Articles
Do I Take?

articles: things

Read

You are a political prisoner who has been **sentenced** to spend the **remainder** of your life on an uninhabited island in the Pacific Ocean (you are 28 years old). The island is 4000 miles from any land, and the chances of escaping are extremely small because of strong ocean **currents**. Fortunately, the island (2000 sq. mi.) has a very moderate climate; temperatures never go below 65 degrees F. in the winter or above 85 degrees F. in the summer. The rainfall on the island is moderate also, about 75 inches spread evenly throughout the year. As a result, there is **lush** vegetation and **diverse** animal life; therefore, food is no problem.

Aside from this, your government has allowed you to take 12 items to the island, and has said that it will provide you with a portable solar generator if you want to take electrical **devices**. The only restrictions are that you may not select a person of the opposite sex to accompany you, and you may not take a **means of** transportation to the island (boat, airplane, etc.).

sentenced: punished by a court

remainder: rest

currents: fast-moving waters

lush: abundant

diverse: varied

devices: appliances

means of: way of

Consider

1. Here are some possible articles to take with you:

a compass	scissors	a radio
an article of clothing	a gun/ammunition	a TV
a telescope	a mirror	a rope
a comb/brush	an axe	a book
a frying pan	a tape recorder	a fishing pole
soap (lifetime supply)	an army knife	a horse
a typewriter	a stove	pencils (lifetime supply)
a deck of cards	a refrigerator	paper (lifetime supply)
a hammer/nails	matches (lifetime supply)	toothbrush/toothpaste
a thermometer	a microscope	(lifetime supply)
antiseptic (lifetime supply)	a large cooking pot	a ball
a lamp (or other source of	cigarettes (lifetime supply)	candles (lifetime supply)
light)	alcoholic drinks (lifetime	a net
sunglasses	supply)	a barometer

2. Remember that you might be able to make many items from the natural resources on the island. For example, you might be able to make an axe from a sharp rock and a stick. Nonetheless, a steel axe might be more reliable and useful.

3. Remember that you are not limited to the list.

4. At least one article you choose *must not* be on the list!

Decide and Write

Article 1: _____

Reason chosen: _____

Article 2: _____

Reason chosen: _____

Article 3: _____

Reason chosen: _____

Article 4: _____

Reason chosen: _____

Article 5: _____

Reason chosen: _____

Article 6: _____

Reason chosen: _____

Article 7: _____

Reason chosen: _____

Article 8: _____

Reason chosen: _____

Article 9: _____

Reason chosen: _____

Article 10: _____

Reason chosen: _____

Article 11: _____

Reason chosen: _____

Article 12: _____

Reason chosen: _____

Discuss

Verbally compare your decisions with those of the classmates in your discussion group. Explain and defend your opinions. Listen carefully to your classmates' opinions, but do not be afraid to disagree with those opinions. Try to reach a group concensus on the best solution to the problem. One person in the group should write down the group's decision.

Extend

1. If you had a choice of remaining on the island and living or trying to leave the island with a 25% chance of escape, which would you choose?

2. Imagine that you have been on the island for 25 years with no contact with the outside world. Suddenly you are saved. What are the first three questions you would ask about the world?

3. What would you miss the most (rank)? _____ magazines, _____ books, _____ tapes, _____ newspapers, _____ TV, _____ movies, _____ radio, _____ telephones.

4. Write a paragraph describing the three books you would take to the island with you. Explain with specific examples.

Which Books to Print?

Read

You are a **book editor** in a large New York City publishing company. Every day you receive at least 10 **manuscripts submitted** by authors who want their works published. Because of your experience, you have developed a **sixth sense** about interesting books and uninteresting books. By **merely** looking at the titles, you can usually get an indication about which books your company should publish and which ones it should not.

In the past three days, 31 manuscripts—whose titles are listed on the following page—have arrived. Make a **preliminary** check and see which 12 books you think will be interesting to the greatest number of people.

book editor: person who chooses what book to publish

manuscripts: unpublished books

submitted: turned in

sixth sense: special idea

merely: only

preliminary: before the final decision

Consider

1. Of course you will read each manuscript completely to **confirm** your feelings about the book.

confirm: make sure of

2. Remember, the titles you choose should be ones the majority of consumers would find interesting, since they will be the people who buy the books.

3. Rank the books in order of your preference.

4. Here are the titles (non-fiction):

The Stock Market Crash of 1987
Music Videos: MTV and VH-1
Moammar Gaddafi: A Biography
The 100 Best Restaurants in the World
The Secret Diary of Albert Einstein
No More Grocery Stores! Grow Your Own Food
Reagan and Gorbachev: Enemies Yet Friends?
Down the Amazon: A Voyage of Discovery
The Complete Book of Dirty Jokes
Life after Death
A Guide to Cheap Vacation Spots in the U.S.
America: Love It or Leave It!
The 1990s: A Terrible Decade for the U.S.?
How to Be Successful with Men
The Story of Philosophy
The CIA and the KGB: Murder for Hire
The Works of Michelangelo: An Appreciation
How to Avoid Cancer
How to Make a Million Dollars
Maradona's Book of Soccer Tips
The Book of Dogs
The Power of the U.S. Media
Television Is Trash!
AIDS!
The Complete Book of Movie Stars
Abortion Is Not Murder!
President Reagan's Secret Love Affairs
The Mysterious Men Who Control the Government
America's Only Native Religion: Mormonism
A Pictorial History of *Playboy* Magazine
How to Live to Be 100

Decide and Write

Title 1: _____

Reason: _____

Title 2: _____

Reason: _____

Title 3: _____

Reason: _____

Title 4: _____

Reason: _____

Title 5: _____

Reason: _____

Title 6: _____

Reason: _____

Title 7: _____

Reason: _____

Title 8: _____

Reason: _____

Title 9: _____

Reason: _____

Title 10: _____

Reason: _____

Title 11: _____

Reason: _____

Title 12: _____

Reason: _____

Discuss

Verbally compare your ideas with those of the classmates in your discussion group. Explain and defend your opinions. Listen carefully to your classmates' opinions, but do not be afraid to disagree with those opinions. Try to reach a group concensus on the best solution to the problem. One person in the group should write down the group's decision.

Extend

1. Is reading important? Do you think that the importance of reading is increasing or decreasing? Explain.

2. What benefits does a person receive from reading books instead of magazines or newspapers?

3. Rate these book forms in your order of enjoyment (1 = most important, 10 = least important):

   _____ romantic books   _____ historical novels   _____ sports books

   _____ science fiction   _____ detective novels   _____ history books

   _____ general novels   _____ scientific books   _____ travel (adventure)

   _____ biographies

4. Do you believe that books will exist in the year 2500? Why or why not?

5. Bring a book to class that you have enjoyed, and share it with the class. Give a 2–3-minute report on it.

Who Gets the Loan?

Read

You are a director in the Loan Department of the First National Bank of Iowa City, Iowa (**assets**: $1 billion). Even though the country is **in the midst of** an **economic recession** and interest rates are high, the number of loan applicants is increasing each month. It is your responsiblity to decide which of the applicants are **good risks** and which are not, and to approve or reject them accordingly.

assets: items of value

in the midst of: in the middle of

economic recession: bad economic period

good risks: people who will pay back loans

Consider

1. The main purpose of the bank is to make money, but it does try to **maintain** the **image** of a responsible community member.

maintain: keep and show

image: public picture

2. The borrower must pay at least 10% of the principal a year. Standard interest rates are 12.5% per year.

3. You can loan part or all of the loan request.

Decide and Write

Loan Applicant 1: Susan and John Jacobs, ages 47 and 48

The Jacobs are hard-working farmers who grow soybeans and cotton. Each year for over 20 years they have borrowed around $500,000 to plant their crops and then have repaid the bank at harvest time. Last year, because of a terrible

drought: lack of water

drought, the Jacobs lost all of their crops and were unable to repay their loan. As a result, they already owe the bank $600,000, and they want to borrow $750,000 more.

Advantages of providing loan: _____

_____

Risks of providing loan: _____

_____

Conclusion: _____

Loan Applicant 2: Walter Gordon, age 30

chronic: uncontrollable

Mr. Gordon has been employed in various positions, but at present he is unemployed and on welfare. As a result of his **chronic** alcoholism, he has a liver illness that necessitates removing the organ. The operation will cost $12,000, but Mr. Gordon has no funds or insurance to cover the cost. Doctors have given him only six months to live if he does not have the operation.

Advantages of providing loan: _____

_____

Risks of providing loan: _____

_____

Conclusion: _____

Loan Applicant 3: Pi-Leng and Jimmy Chan, ages 53 and 55

The Chans have just immigrated to the United States from Hong Kong. They have no credit record in the United States, but they were successful restaurant owners in Hong Kong. Neither of them presently has a job; nonetheless, they have deposited $40,000 of their savings at your bank. They would like to borrow $50,000 to open a new Chinese restaurant in town.

Advantages of providing loan: _____

_____

Risks of providing loan: _____

_____

Conclusion: _____

Loan Applicant 4: David Max, age 16

Mr. Max, a high school student, has a reputation as a mathematical genius, having won awards throughout the nation. He also has been an amateur inventor and has recently developed a solar-powered car! His invention has been tested by experts, who think it is workable. Max is applying for a $15,000 loan to build two **prototypes** of the car.

prototypes: models

Advantages of providing loan: _____

_____

Risks of providing loan: _____

_____

Conclusion: _____

Loan Applicant 5: Peter and Roberta Hayes, ages 41 and 39

The Hayes have one child. Since their marriage 16 years ago, they have been saving their money for a down payment on a house. During that time they have lived in a trailer and three different apartments. Recently, Pete was promoted to become assistant manager of the grocery store in which he works ($17,000 a year salary), and Roberta is an **R.N.** at the local hospital (salary of $22,000 a year). They want to borrow $60,000 for a $75,000 house ($15,000 down payment).

R.N.: Registered Nurse

Advantages of providing loan: _____

_____

Risks of providing loan: _____

_____

Conclusion: _____

Loan Applicant 6: Steven Saliba, age 23

Mr. Saliba has just graduated from Iowa State University with a Master's degree in Business Administration (MBA). While at the university, Saliba had the idea of beginning a new nationwide telephone/video service. Mr. Saliba's service would provide telephone users with the capability of seeing the people they are talking with. He would like $100,000 to get his service started in Iowa City.

Advantages of providing loan: _____

_____

Risks of providing loan: _____

_____

Conclusion: _____

Loan Applicant 7: Jason Anders, age 45

outstanding loans: loans that have not yet been paid

Mr. Anders is a multi-millionaire real-estate developer in your area who has had numerous successful loans with your bank. At present he has two **outstanding loans** from the bank in the sum of $890,000. He has an excellent credit record and now wants to borrow $600,000 more to help finance his new shopping center.

Advantages of providing loan: _____

_____

Risks of providing loan: _____

_____

Conclusion: _____

Loan Applicant 8: John Harris, age 19

Mr. Harris' father is dead, and his mother works full time as a waitress to support the other five children in the family. Mr. Harris himself worked part time throughout high school to help his mother. Now he is requesting a $20,000 loan to finance his four years of undergraduate school.

Advantages of providing loan: _____

_____

Risks of providing loan: _____

_____

Conclusion: _____

Discuss

Verbally compare your decisions with those of the classmates in your discussion group. Explain and defend your opinions. Listen carefully to your classmates' opinions, but do not be afraid to disagree with those opinions. Try to reach a group concensus on the best solution to the problem. One person in the group should write down the group's decision.

Extend

1. In general, what is your opinion of banks—trustworthy or not? helpful to the community or not? necessary?

2. In some Arab countries, it is against the law for a bank to charge interest (or for a customer to receive interest). What do you think of this system?

3. It seems as if cash is slowly being replaced by credit cards and computer transactions. Will cash ever become **obsolete**? Explain.   **obsolete:** no longer used

4. Do you think that banks in developed countries should lend money to Third World nations already deeply in debt? Explain.

5. At this moment, you probably have money in a bank. Why? How did you choose your bank?

Into the Future!

Read

Imagine that you had been born in 1880 and had lived to 1960. You would have seen an incredible number of changes in your lifetime. It is doubtful that many people in 1880 could have predicted that by 1960 men would be in space.

Now a similar situation is confronting you: You have been asked to predict what the world will be like in 2025. More specifically, what do you think will be the 15 biggest changes that will take place in your lifetime? And will those changes make the world better or worse?

Consider

You should consider physical changes in the world as well as technological **advances**.

advances:
accomplishments

Decide and Write

Change 1: _____

Positive or Negative Effect: _____

Change 2: _____

Positive or Negative Effect: _____

Change 3: _____

Positive or Negative Effect: _____

Change 4: _____

Positive or Negative Effect: _____

Change 5: _____

Positive or Negative Effect: _____

Change 6: _____

Positive or Negative Effect: _____

Change 7: _____

Positive or Negative Effect: _____

Change 8: _____

Positive or Negative Effect: _____

Change 9: _____

Positive or Negative Effect: _____

Change 10: _____

Positive or Negative Effect: _____

Change 11: _____

Positive or Negative Effect: _____

Change 12: _____

Positive or Negative Effect: _____

Change 13: _____

Positive or Negative Effect: _____

Change 14: _____

Positive or Negative Effect: _____

Change 15: _____

Positive or Negative Effect: _____

Discuss

Verbally compare your decisions with those of the classmates in your discussion group. Explain and defend your opinions. Listen carefully to your classmates' opinions, but do not be afraid to disagree with those opinions. Try to reach a group concensus on the best solution to the problem. One person in the group should write down the group's decision.

Extend

1. In general, are you optimistic or pessimistic about the future? Why?

2. More specifically, is human civilization advancing or declining? What indications do you see to support your idea?

3. At present, the U. S. and the USSR are the two most powerful countries in the world. After looking at a map, choose which *five* countries will be most powerful in the year 2500.

4. Using your artistic ability, draw a picture of what you imagine a human being will look like one million years from today.

5. Write a composition about three positive trends you see taking place in the world today.

Writing a Short Constitution and a Bill of Rights

Read

You are members of the **governing council** of a new country that has just been established on the uninhabited planet Nebula in the year 2113. The planet has a **temperate** climate, a tremendous amount of raw materials, and **ample** land for agriculture. Your problem is to write a short constitution and a **bill of rights** that establish the **principles** by which you and your 5000 **settlers** from earth will be governed.

governing council: group of leaders

temperate: moderate

ample: enough

bill of rights: specific list of what citizens can do

principles: ideas

settlers: first people to live in a place

Consider

1. The 5000 settlers make a very heterogeneous group; many different races, nationalities, and philosophies are represented.

2. The settlers have left earth because of overpopulated conditions on their home planet.

3. Be specific with your wording of the documents so that there is no **ambiguity**.

ambiguity: vagueness

Decide and Write

I. CONSTITUTION (Fill in the blanks)

We, the people of _____ , have come to Nebula
                              (name of country)

for the purpose of establishing a new country based on the principles of

_____ , _____ , and
          (noun)   (noun)

_____ . We firmly believe that all people _____
          (noun)

_____ . Furthermore, we believe

that _____ .

For these reasons, we will attempt to make this a country in which

_____ .

To accomplish this, we dedicate all our energies.

II. BILL OF RIGHTS FOR THE CITIZENS AND THE GOVERNMENT OF

_____ .
                              (name of country)

1. Each citizen of our country shall have the right to _____

_____ .

2. Each citizen of our country shall have the right to _____

_____ .

3. The government may not pass a law that _____

_____ .

4. The government may not pass a law that _____

_____ .

5. The government may not pass a law that _____

_____ .

6. The government does have the right to _____

_____ .

7. The government does have the right to _____

_____ .

8. The government does have the right to _____

_____ .

9. It is the responsibility of the government to always _____

_____ .

10. It is the responsibility of the citizens to always _____

_____ .

11. _____

_____ .

Discuss

Verbally compare your decisions with those of the classmates in your discussion group. Explain and defend your opinions. Listen carefully to your classmates' opinions, but do not be afraid to disagree with those opinions. Try to reach a group consensus on the best solution to the problem. One person in the group should write down the group's decision.

Extend

1. When settlers begin a new country, what are the biggest problems that they will usually face?

2. Would you like to be the leader of your country? Would you like to work for the government of your country? Explain.

3. The United States Constitution has a Bill of Rights with 10 rights specifically stated. Discuss whether you think these four rights are good for all countries:

   1. The **press** shall have complete freedom.
   2. Every person is free to speak about any subject.
   3. The country shall not have an official religion.
   4. Because it is important to defend a country, each citizen has the right to have guns.

press: newspapers, TV, radio, magazines

Who is Responsible, and for How Much?

Read

You are a member of a California jury trying to decide the result of a **civil suit** brought by Ms. Melissa Brown. These are the basic facts: On the night of December 31, Ms. Brown, a 29-year-old third-year medical student, was returning home from a New Year's Eve party.

At approximately 12:45 AM, her Ford Pinto was hit **from the rear** by a Cadillac Seville driven by Mr. James Jones, a 56-year-old millionaire vice-president of a local architectural firm.

According to the testimony at the trial, Mr. Jones' car was traveling 15 miles over the speed limit when it went out of control and hit Ms. Brown's car on an icy, poorly lit street. The resulting collision caused the Pinto to crumple and its gas tank caught fire.

Ms. Brown suffered third-degree burns over the top half of her body, completely **disfiguring** her face and paralyzing her from the neck down. Doctors say she will probably never be able to move that part of her body again unless she receives extensive medical help. For these reasons, and others below, Ms. Brown filed the largest civil suit in U.S. history—$25 million—against the **parties** named below.

The trial has lasted three weeks. Now you must decide how much money, if any, to award.

civil suit: non-criminal legal action

from the rear: in the back

disfiguring: changing the shape of

parties: defendants

Consider

1. The trial evidence established that Ms. Brown had an excellent driving record (no convictions of any type), and was driving completely within the law at the time of the accident.

sobriety test: test for drunkenness

under the influence: drunk

2. The trial record also established that Mr. Jones was legally drunk at the time of the accident (according to a **sobriety test**). It was the second time he had been involved in an accident while driving **under the influence** (in the previous accident, no one was injured).

Decide and Write

Ms. Brown has sued the following:

treacherous: very dangerous

given a one year suspended sentence: not required to go to prison

1. **Mr. James Jones.** Mr. Jones' drunkenness undoubtedly led him to exceed the speed limit and affected his ability to react to **treacherous** street conditions. As a result of the accident, he was found guilty in criminal court of ''negligent contribution to an accident'' and **given a one-year suspended sentence**.

   Amount of money Mr. Jones must pay Ms. Brown: _____

   Reason: _____

patron: customer
premises: area

2. **The Disco Bar.** According to California law, the owner of a bar can be held legally responsible for allowing a drunk **patron** to leave the **premises**. Mr. Jones had been drinking at the Disco Bar for four hours prior to the accident. Testimony revealed that the manager of the bar knew Mr. Jones was drunk and did nothing.

   Amount of money the Disco Bar must pay Ms. Brown _____

   Reason: _____

3. **The City of Los Angeles, Maintenance Department.** At the time of the accident, though unusual, snow had been falling for six hours. According to testimony, the Department had made no attempt either to clear the streets or to post warning signs.

Amount the Department must pay Ms. Brown: _____

Reason: _____

4. **The City of Los Angeles, Lighting Department.** The Department had never provided adequate lighting in the area despite previous promises to do so. In the area where Ms. Brown's accident occurred, the city's average accident rate is exceeded by more than 15 percent.

Amount the Department must pay Ms. Brown: _____

Reason: _____

5. **The Ford Motor Co.** Tests of all models of the Ford Pinto **revealed** a **critical deficiency** in the structural design that made it easier for the gas tank to **rupture** on contact. Ford **allegedly** knew of the defect, yet did nothing. Over 500 similar accidents have been reported nationwide.

revealed: showed
critical deficiency: serious problem
rupture: break open
allegedly: supposedly

Amount Ford must pay Ms. Brown: _____

Reason: _____

6. **The Harper Aluminum Co.** According to strict regulations, the bumpers of cars must be built to withstand an impact at 35 miles per hour (mph) without crumpling. Mr. Jones was going approximately 35 mph in a 20 mph zone when the accident occurred. Nonetheless, the rear bumper of the Pinto crumpled immediately, allowing the gas tank to be exposed.

Amount Harper must pay Ms. Brown: _____

Reason: _____

verify: check

7. **The Department of Health, Education and Welfare (HEW), Washington D.C.** This Department has the legal responsibility to **verify** that all car models are free from structural defects. Apparently, inspectors were negligent in checking the Pinto bumper and gas tank.

   Amount HEW must pay Ms. Brown: _____

   Reason: _____

8. **The State of California, Department of Motor Vehicles, Inspection Division.** This Division is authorized by the State to retest for structural defects any and every vehicle that is sold in the State. This was not done in the case of the Ford Pinto because of administrative error.

   Amount the State of California must pay Ms. Brown: _____

   Reason: _____

Discuss

Verbally compare your decisions with those of the classmates in your discussion group. Explain and defend your opinions. Listen carefully to your classmates' opinions, but do not be afraid to disagree with those opinions. Try to reach a group consensus on the best solution to the problem. One person in the group should write down the group's decision.

Extend

1. Many states are now passing laws that limit the amount of money a victim can receive for injuries. Do you believe that such awards should be limited?

2. Should a bar owner be legally responsible if a person gets drunk at his or her bar, drives away in a car, and kills someone in a traffic accident?

3. Bhopal, India . . . Chernobyl, USSR . . . Minamata, Japan . . . Throughout the world, governments and corporations are being held responsible for accidents that cause injuries and fatalities. How can citizens make governments and corporations act more responsibly?

4. Imagine either that you are handicapped and confined to a wheelchair or that you are not handicapped or confined. Write a composition about life from your chosen point of view.

Design a Product and an Advertising Campaign

Read

You belong to an advertising agency that specializes in marketing new products. You have just received a **"rush"** project: Revlon has decided to create a new perfume. It is your responsibility to design the product and plan a **marketing campaign**.

"rush": must be finished fast

marketing campaign: selling plan

Consider

1. Traditionally, women have been the primary buyers of perfume; but men have recently begun buying more perfume. Therefore, try to design your product to **appeal to** the greatest number of people.

appeal to: attract

2. As always, the chief goal of any large business is making money. Therefore, try to get the most for the corporation's money.

Decide and Write

New Product Design

1. Name of new perfume: _____

2. Color of new perfume (clear is a possibility): _____

3. Smell of new perfume (circle one): very sweet, sweet, slightly sweet, neutral

4. Type of container (circle one): plastic container, glass bottle

5. Shape of container (draw): _____

6. Quantity of perfume in container (only one size, in ounces): _____

7. Color of container (clear is a possibility): _____

8. Type of dispenser (circle one): pump spray, no pump

9. Design the label to appear on the front of the box that holds the perfume container.

   A. Size _____

   B. Fill in the label as you want it to appear.

   [ ]

10. Projected cost of perfume per ounce: _____

Marketing Campaign

1. Create a **catchy slogan** for your perfume:

   catchy: lively

   slogan: short phrase

   _____

   _____

2. Type of markets campaign is **aimed toward** (circle three):

   aimed toward: trying to get

teenage girls	men ages 36–50
teenage boys	women ages 36–50
men ages 20–35	men ages 50 +
women ages 20–35	women ages 50 +

3. What percentage of the advertising budget will you spend on each of the following?

   newspapers _____   television _____

   magazines _____   free mailing samples _____

   radio _____   other _____ : _____

4. In what types of magazines will you advertise?

   _____

5. On what types of radio and TV programs will you buy advertising time?

   _____

6. How many free samples will you mail? _____

7. Create and perform a 30-second TV commercial for the perfume:

_____

_____

_____

_____

_____

Discuss

Verbally compare your decisions with those of the classmates in your discussion group. Explain and defend your opinions. Listen carefully to your classmates' opinions, but do not be afraid to disagree with those opinions. Try to reach a group consensus on the best solution to the problem. One person in the group should write down the group's decision.

Extend

1. Are you influenced by advertising? For example, when you go to the grocery store do you buy products that you've seen or read about? Give examples.

2. What kind of deodorant do you use? Why?

3. How does TV advertising differ from newspaper or magazine advertising? Which do you think is most effective?

4. Look through several newspapers and magazines. Cut out and bring to class the three best advertisements you find. Explain why they appeal to you.

Whom Do We Admit to Medical School?

Read

The Harvard University Medical School admits 100 new students each year. This year, as in all previous years, the number of applicants exceeds the number of spaces. Based on preliminary decisions, 96 out of the 100 spaces have been filled.

However, there are eight applicants still in the running for the four remaining **spots**. Listed below you will find a short biographical sketch of the eight applicants. Choose the four you feel are best qualified for admission to the Medical School.

spots: positions

Consider

1. The University is committed to **affirmative action**; there can be no discrimination based on sex.

2. When all other factors have been equal, past admissions committees have made a comparative list of MCAT (Medical College Admission Test) and GPA (Grade Point Average) scores. Whether this is done this year is completely at your **discretion**. One such list of this year's applicants appears here; you may fill in the GPA-University list if you feel it is necessary.

affirmative action: policy to give a certain percentage of positions to minority students

discretion: choice

Applicant	MCAT	GPA-University (Name)
Collinswood	896	
Poitier	895	

123

Applicant	MCAT	GPA-University (Name)
Heggi	890	
Morgan	888	
Nagai	885	
Ankermajian	882	
Townshend	876	
Kruger	870	

Decide and Write

Applicant 1: Qais Heggi, age 26, Master of Science in Physiology from the University of Cairo

equivalent of: same as

Mr. Heggi had the **equivalent of** a 3.9 GPA at Cairo (out of a possible 4.0), and he scored 890 (out of a possible 900) on the MCAT. He also worked for one year as a medical assistant at the Cairo Teaching Hospital. On his application he writes, ''I want to become a doctor so I can return to my native country of Oman and help relieve the shortage of experienced doctors there.''

Reasons in favor of acceptance: _____

Reasons in favor of rejection: _____

Conclusion of committee: _____

Applicant 2: Mary Townshend, age 23, Master of Nuclear Technology from MIT

Ms. Townshend had a perfect 4.0 GPA at MIT, and she scored 876 on the MCAT. While doing her graduate work at MIT, she directed a research team that made outstanding **breakthroughs** in the use of nuclear technology to remove **tumors**. She writes, ''I believe that the medical expertise and facilities available at Harvard will be of incalculable help as I continue researching ways to **eradicate** cancer.''

breakthroughs: advances
tumors: cancers

eradicate: eliminate

Reasons in favor of acceptance: _____

Reasons in favor of rejection: _____

Conclusion of committee: _____

Applicant 3: Gilles Poitier, age 24, Master of Science in Anatomy from the Sorbonne in Paris

Mr. Poitier had the equivalent of a 3.85 GPA at the Sorbonne, and he scored 895 on the MCAT. Mr. Poitier took two years off from school to work as a medical assistant in the desert region of Algeria. According to his statement, he "wishes to return to a developing country to practice medicine."

Reasons in favor of acceptance: _____

Reasons in favor of rejection: _____

Conclusion of committee: _____

Applicant 4: Johann Kruger, age 24, Master of Science and Ph.D. in Pathology from the University of South Africa, Capetown

Mr. Kruger had the equivalent of a 3.95 GPA, and he scored 870 on the MCAT. While working on his graduate degrees, he was an **intern** at Groote Schuur Hospital, where he worked with Dr. Christian Barnard, the pioneer of heart transplant surgery. Barnard highly recommends Kruger, who writes that he wishes "to specialize in cardiology at Harvard."

intern: assistant doctor

Reasons in favor of acceptance: _____

Reasons in favor of rejection: _____

Conclusion of committee: _____

Applicant 5: Sarah Collinswood, age 25, Master of Science in Biochemistry from Oxford University, England

Ms. Collinswood had the equivalent of a 3.82 GPA, and she scored 896 on the MCAT. Her master's thesis at Oxford was the **brilliant** and widely **acclaimed** "A DNA Approach to Fighting Disease." She hopes to "increase my understanding of the body's biochemical composition so that I can continue to learn more about man's natural disease-fighting mechanisms."

brilliant: very intelligent
acclaimed: recognized

Reasons in favor of acceptance: _____

Reasons in favor of rejection: _____

Conclusion of committee: _____

Applicant 6: Bill Ankermajian, age 20, Bachelor of Science in Biological Sciences from Stanford, Master of Science in Physiology from Harvard

Mr. Ankermajian had a perfect 4.0 GPA throughout college, and made 882 on the MCAT. Harvard Professor Emeritus Philip Jones considers Ankermajian ''one of the two or three most innovative thinkers I've ever taught.'' Ankermajian writes that he believes ''my talents could best be realized in the field of surgery.''

Reasons in favor of acceptance: _____

Reasons in favor of rejection: _____

Conclusion of committee: _____

Applicant 7: Shuichi Nagai, age 24, Master of Science in General Medicine from Tokyo University

Mr. Nagai had the equivalent of a 3.97 at Tokyo, and he scored 885 on the MCAT. He has worked as an intern for one year at Tokyo General Hospital and has published two articles in the *Harvard Medical Review* describing ways to treat **neurological** disorders. He wishes ''to continue my research in the neurological field.''

neurological: having to do with the nervous system

Reasons in favor of acceptance: _____

Reasons in favor of rejection: _____

Conclusion of committee: _____

Applicant 8: Vanessa Morgan, age 27, Bachelor of Science from the University of Chicago, Master of Science from the University of California, Berkeley, Ph.D. in Anatomy from Johns Hopkins University

Ms. Morgan had a 3.91 GPA at Berkeley and Johns Hopkins, and she scored 888 on the MCAT. She is already recognized as an expert in the limited field of bone-marrow diseases, and she writes that she wishes ''to expand my knowledge to the broad area of all bone disorders.''

Reasons in favor of acceptance: _____

Reasons in favor of rejection: _____

Conclusion of committee: _____

Discuss

Verbally compare your decisions with those of the classmates in your discussion group. Explain and defend your opinions. Listen carefully to your classmates' opinions, but do not be afraid to disagree with those opinions. Try to reach a group consensus on the best solution to the problem. One person in the group should write down the group's decision.

Extend

1. MCAT, TOEFL, GRE, SAT—Do universities put too much emphasis on tests? Explain.

2. Do you think the TOEFL test is a good test of English? What does the TOEFL test not include?

3. What is your opinion of affirmative action? How can institutions try to correct the effects of past discrimination?

4. Role play: With a partner, write and act out an interview between a university entrance officer and a prospective student.

The 15 Most Important People in History

Read

Incredible! A **fleet** of space ships has just landed on Earth. The space beings are friendly, and they would like to learn about Earth history. These space people believe they can understand Earth if they learn about its most important leaders. They want you to provide a list of the 15 most important people who have lived in the last 4000 years.

fleet: group

Consider

1. These 15 people may not necessarily be the most famous people in history. They should be chosen because of the impact they have had on human culture.

2. You must choose at least three people who are not on the following list.

3. Here is a list of possibilities:

Political and Military Leaders
Alexander the Great (356–323 B.C.): Macedonian conqueror of much of the known world
Simon Bolivar (1783–1830): Venezuelan liberator of much of South America
Napoleon Bonaparte (1769–1821): French conqueror of central Europe
Augustus Caesar (27 B.C.–14 A.D.): Roman Emperor at the height of the Roman Empire
Dwight Eisenhower (1890–1969): Allied Army Commander, World War II
Elizabeth Tudor (1553–1603): Queen of England during the age of colonization
Thomas Jefferson (1743–1826): Writer of the U.S. Declaration of Independence
Jomo Kenyatta (1893–1978): African political leader
Genghis Khan (1167–1227): Mongolian conqueror of Asia and eastern Europe
Adolf Hitler (1889–1945): German dictator who started World War II
Vladimir Lenin (1870–1924): Founder of the USSR
Mao Tse-tung (1893–1976): Founder of the People's Republic of China

Artists
Ludwig van Beethoven (1770–1827): German composer
Michelangelo Buonarroti (1475–1564): Italian artist and sculptor
Pablo Picasso (1881–1973): Spanish **initiator** of modern art
Leonardo da Vinci (1452–1519): Italian painter, sculptor, scientist, inventor
Wolfgang A. Mozart (1756–1791): Austrian composer

initiator: beginner

Philosphers and Religionists
Aristotle (384–322 B.C.): Greek philosopher and scientist
Buddha (563–483 B.C.): Indian philosopher, founder of Buddhism
Confucius (559–471 B.C.): Chinese philosopher
Mohandas Gandhi (1869–1949): Indian philosopher
Jesus (1 A.D.–34 A.D.): Founder of Christianity
Moses (14th century B.C.): Jewish leader who received the 10 Commandments
Karl Marx (1818–1883): German philosopher
Mohammed (570–632): Arabic founder of Islam
Plato (427–347 B.C.): Greek philosopher
Lao-Tzu (604–531 B.C.): Chinese founder of Taoism

Scientists
Howard Aiken (1900–1973): U.S. mathematician who designed the first large computer
Niels Bohr (1885–1962): Danish physicist, developer of quantum theory
Marie Curie (1867–1935): Polish chemist, renowned for work on radium
Charles Darwin (1809–1882): British naturalist, developed theory of evolution
Albert Einstein (1879–1955): German-American, developer of theory of relativity
Alexander Fleming (1881–1955): British bacteriologist, discovered penicillin
Sigmund Freud (1856–1939): Austrian founder of psychoanalysis
Galileo (1564–1642): Italian astronomer, founder of the experimental method
Hippocrates (460–377 B.C.): Greek, called the "Father of Medicine"
Johannes Kepler (1571–1630): German discoverer of the laws of planetary motion
Al-Khwarizmi (780–850): Arabian mathematician who developed algebra
Antoine Lavoisier (1743–1794): French founder of modern chemistry
Gregor Mendel (1822–1884): Austrian founder of genetics

Isaac Newton (1642–1727): British discoverer of the laws of motion and gravitation

Hideyo Noguchi (1876–1928): Japanese bacteriologist renowned in many areas

William Roentgen (1845–1923): German discoverer of x-rays

Abdullah Ibn Sina (Avicenna) (979–1037): Arabian physician who helped lay the basis of modern medicine

Businessmen

Henry Ford (1863–1947): American mass producer of cars

John D. Rockefeller (1839–1937): American who founded the first oil company

Sheikh Ahmed Yamani (?–   ): Saudi, former leader of OPEC

Explorers

Christopher Columbus (1446–1506): Italian who traveled to America

Ferdinand Magellan (1480–1521): Portuguese navigator, first to circumnavigate the world

Marco Polo (1254–1324): Italian who first journeyed to China

Inventors

Alexander G. Bell (1847–1922): Scottish inventor of the telephone

Thomas Edison (1847–1931): U.S. inventor of the incandescent lamp, phonograph

Johann Gutenberg (1398–1463): German inventor of the printing press

Anton van Leeuwenhoek (1632–1723): Dutch inventor of the microscope

Alfred Nobel (1833–1896): Swedish inventor of dynamite

Orville (1871–1948) and Wilbur (1867–1912) Wright: U.S. inventors of the airplane

Decide and Write

Person 1: _____

Reason: _____

Person 2: _____

Reason: _____

Person 3: _____

Reason: _____

Person 4: _____

Reason: _____

Person 5: _____

Reason: _____

Person 6: _____

Reason: _____

Person 7: _____

Reason: _____

Person 8: _____

Reason: _____

Person 9: _____

Reason: _____

Person 10: _____

Reason: _____

Person 11: _____

Reason: _____

Person 12: _____

Reason: _____

Person 13: _____

Reason: _____

Person 14: _____

Reason: _____

Person 15: _____

Reason: _____

Discuss

Verbally compare your decisions with those of the classmates in your discussion group. Explain and defend your opinions. Listen carefully to your classmates' opinions, but do not be afraid to disagree with those opinions. Try to reach a group consensus on the best solution to the problem. One person in the group should write down the group's decision.

Extend

1. What makes a great person? In other words, what characteristics do great people generally have in common?

2. Who is the most famous person in the history of your country? Would you like to be famous some day?

3. A well-known expression is that "Fame is fleeting." What does this mean? Why is it usually true?

4. Are there any people alive today who you think will be famous in 2000 years? If so, who?

5. If you could be one person in history, who would it be? Write a composition explaining your choice.

How Do We Respond?

Read

You are a Politburo member of the USSR. Your General Secretary has just received emergency word that a small, underdeveloped country that is an **ally** of the United States has **seized** one of your country's spy ships.

    The ship is now held in the **harbor** of that country, and its crew of 56 men will be **tried** on charges of **espionage** (which carry a death penalty). The General Secretary has asked you to look at the following options, give him the advantages and disadvantages of each option, and then rank the options in the order of your preference (1 = most preferred, 8 = least preferred).

ally: friend
seized: taken control of
harbor: protected water
tried: taken to court
espionage: spying

Consider

1. The spy ship contained super-secret material that could be disastrous in the hands of your capitalist **adversary**.

    adversary: enemy

2. According to neutral ships in the area, your vessel did **violate** the territorial waters of the small country.

    violate: trespass

Decide and Write

Option A. Direct military **intervention**: Send your country's **troops** to the country to seize the ship and recover the men.

intervention: action
troops: soldiers

Advantages: _____

Disadvantages: _____

Rank of preference: _____

135

seize: forcibly take

Option B. Direct military intervention: Order one of your allies in the area to send its troops to the country to **seize** the ship and recover the men.

Advantages: _____

Disadvantages: _____

Rank of preference: _____

Option C. Send the small country a letter of regret, admit responsibility for the spy ship, and request the return of the ship and the crew.

Advantages: _____

Disadvantages: _____

Rank of preference: _____

Option D. Send the country a letter demanding return of the ship and men at once. Warn that they otherwise will "face the consequences" of their action.

Advantages: _____

Disadvantages: _____

Rank of preference: _____

Option E. Report the incident to the United Nations: Claim the ship was a merchant ship, and ask the U.N. to demand its return.

Advantages: _____

Disadvantages: _____

Rank of preference: _____

Option F. Seize a ship and its crew belonging to the country that has your country's ship, and hold it until your ship and crew are released.

Advantages: _____

Disadvantages: _____

Option G. Contact your superpower enemy and demand that they return the ship, warning that failure to do so will increase tensions between the two countries.

Advantages: _____

Disadvantages: _____

Rank of preference: _____

Option H. Take no action on the matter.

Advantages: _____

Disadvantages: _____

Rank of preference: _____

Discuss

Verbally compare your decisions with those of the classmates in your discussion group. Explain and defend your opinions. Listen carefully to your classmates' opinions, but do not be afraid to disagree with those opinions. Try to reach a group consensus on the best solution to the problem. One person in the group should write down the group's decision.

Extend

1. What is the main problem between the U.S. and the USSR? Why can't the two strongest countries in the world talk about peace instead of war?

2. What is your opinion of the United Nations: helpful? useless?

3. In what cases is a country justified in using military force?

4. In today's world, is it possible for a country to be neutral? How would you describe your country's attitudes toward the U.S. and toward the USSR?

5. Make a list of 10 questions about the USSR; use them to interview an American. Write a short report based on his or her answers.

Which Items Do You Think Are Representative of the U.S. Today?

Read

The city of New Orleans, Louisiana, has decided to construct a new city administration building. The Mayor thinks it would be a good idea to follow tradition and place a **time capsule** inside the **cornerstone**. The time capsule, which will be opened 200 years from now, will give the people of the future an idea of life in the United States today.

As a member of the New Orleans Historical Commission, you have been given the job of selecting 12 items that will be placed in the box ($3' \times 3' \times 3'$).

time capsule: container with historical items in it

cornerstone: part of building that contains time capsule

Consider

1. Remember that the articles in the box are to be representative only of present U.S. culture, not of world conditions.

2. Remember that size is a factor; you cannot choose something so large that it will not fit in the box.

3. The following is a list of possibilities. You must choose at least two items that are not on the list:

a quart of oil
a movie starring _____
an American English dictionary
a computer chip from the most
    sophisticated American computer
a handgun
a ticket to Disneyland
an empty box of Kentucky Fried
    Chicken
a videotape of the Number 1 TV show
a pillbox of **tranquilizers**
a pair of running shoes
a pornographic magazine
a test tube
a sample of water from the Mississippi
    River

a Bible
a bumper sticker reading: ''Say No to
    Drugs''
the keys to a car
the new record by _____
an advertisement page of a newspaper
    listing food prices
a pair of worn-out blue jeans
a football helmet
a book entitled _____
a T-shirt with ''Gay Rights'' printed on it
a telephone directory of _____
a sack of garbage from the house of a
    middle-class family
the most recent **State of the Union
    message** by the President

tranquilizers: pills that
help one relax

**State of the Union
message:** annual speech
to the U.S. Congress
about the country

Decide and Write

Item 1: _____

Reason: _____

Item 2: _____

Reason: _____

Item 3: _____

Reason: _____

Item 4: _____

Reason: _____

Item 5: _____

Reason: _____

Item 6: _____

Reason: _____

Item 7: _____

Reason: _____

Item 8: _____

Reason: _____

Item 9: _____

Reason: _____

Item 10: _____

Reason: _____

Item 11: _____

Reason: _____

Item 12: _____

Reason: _____

Discuss

Verbally compare your decisions with those of the classmates in your discussion group. Explain and defend your opinions. Listen carefully to your classmates' opinions, but do not be afraid to disagree with those opinions. Try to reach a group consensus on the best solution to the problem. One person in the group should write down the group's decision.

Extend

1. People who come from very old countries, such as India and China, often say that the U.S. has no culture. What do you think? How would you describe American culture?

2. Considering the well-publicized problems of American society, why do so many people immigrate to the U.S.?

3. Why did you (or, would you like to) come to the United States to study?

4. Rate these in importance to Americans (1 = important, 5 = not important):

   _____ family   _____ religion   _____ money

   _____ happiness   _____ education

5. There are many countries that export products, but the U.S. is one of the few countries that export culture. What American ideas/products appeal to people in other countries?

Starting a
New Civilization

civilization: society and
culture

Read

A nuclear war has just taken place! Soon, most of the world will be destroyed
by radiation. However, you, the **delegates to** the United Nations, have just
learned that due to unusual wind patterns one small, uninhabited island 300
miles off the coast of Australia will not be completely destroyed. Scientists
think that the plants on the island will be damaged, but the soil will not be
ruined.

Unfortunately, there is only time enough for one small airplane at an
Australian airport to make it to the island. **Aside from** the pilot, the plane can
carry only six people. But there are 10 people at the airport who want to get on
the airplane. As delegates to the U.N., you have one hour to decide which *six*
of the following people will live and which *four* must die.

delegates to: members of

ruined: spoiled

aside from: in addition to

Consider

Remember as you decide on a basis for selecting people that the six people you
choose will have to start a new civilization.

Decide and Write

Possible Survivor 1: A man of religion (age unknown)

Reasons in favor of survival: _____

Reasons against survival: _____

Conclusion of committee: _____

Possible Survivor 2: A homosexual doctor (male, age 46)

Reasons in favor of survival: _____

Reasons against survival: _____

Conclusion of committee: _____

Possible Survivor 3: A female singer (age 30)

Reasons in favor of survival: _____

Reasons against survival: _____

Conclusion of committee: _____

Possible Survivor 4: A policeman with a gun (age unknown)

Reasons in favor of survival: _____

Reasons against survival: _____

Conclusion of committee: _____

Possible Survivor 5: The **chief** of an African tribe (age unknown)   **chief:** leader

Reasons in favor of survival: _____

Reasons against survival: _____

Conclusion of committee: _____

Possible Survivor 6: The chief's pregnant wife (age unknown)

Reasons in favor of survival: _____

Reasons against survival: _____

Conclusion of committee: _____

Possible Survivor 7: A judge (male, age 41)

Reasons in favor of survival: _____

Reasons against survival: _____

Conclusion of committee: _____

Possible Survivor 8: A university professor (female, age 34)

Reasons in favor of survival: _____

Reasons against survival: _____

Conclusion of committee: _____

Possible Survivor 9: A **warrior** (with a **spear**) from a nearby South Pacific island (male, age unknown)

warrior: person responsible for protecting or fighting

spear: hunting weapon

Reasons in favor of survival: _____

Reasons against survival: _____

Conclusion of committee: _____

Possible Survivor 10: An alcoholic agricultural scientist (female, age unknown)

Reasons in favor of survival: _____

Reasons against survival: _____

Conclusion of committee: _____

Discuss

Verbally compare your decisions with those of the classmates in your discussion group. Explain and defend your opinions. Listen carefully to your classmates' opinions, but do not be afraid to disagree with those opinions. Try to reach a group consensus on the best solution to the problem. One person in the group should write down the group's decision.

Extend

1. Do you think that a nuclear war is likely in the next 50 years? Give reasons for your answer.

2. List three results of a possible nuclear war. What do you think the chances of survival would be?

3. What should governments do to avoid the possibility of a nuclear war? What can individuals do?

4. Look in some recent newspapers, and cut out all of the articles you can find about nuclear war. Report on one of them to the class.

5. Imagine that a nuclear war has taken place and that you are the only survivor. Write a paragraph describing your situation, including a description of the environment and a discussion of your feelings.

Unsolvable Problems

Read

Throughout this book you have been asked to solve problems. However, there are surely some problems that cannot be solved and questions that cannot be answered. We might classify these questions into two types: philosophical questions and questions about the physical universe.

Philosophical **inquiries** seldom seem to be solved satisfactorily. For example, philosophers have asked ''What is beauty?'' for thousands of years, but have never been able to provide an answer.

inquiries: questions

Technology often provides us with an answer to the second type of question. For example, people asked the question, ''What is the atmosphere composed of on Mars?'' Others then invented the technology necessary to send a spaceship to Mars to discover the answer. However, other questions—such as ''What causes cancer?''—have yet to be answered.

As the final problem in this book, try to think of 15 important questions or problems in the physical universe that may never be solved (or that will present the greatest difficulty to researchers).

Consider

Try to approach the problem **systematically**. Consider each possible area containing problems or difficulties, such as medicine, geology.

systematically: in an organized way

Decide and Write

Question 1: _____

Reason for difficulty: _____

Question 2: _____

Reason for difficulty: _____

Question 3: _____

Reason for difficulty: _____

Question 4: _____

Reason for difficulty: _____

Question 5: _____

Reason for difficulty: _____

Question 6: _____

Reason for difficulty: _____

Question 7: _____

Reason for difficulty: _____

Question 8: _____

Reason for difficulty: _____

Question 9: _____

Reason for difficulty: _____

Question 10: _____

Reason for difficulty: _____

Question 11: _____

Reason for difficulty: _____

Question 12: _____

Reason for difficulty: _____

Question 13: _____

Reason for difficulty: _____

Question 14: _____

Reason for difficulty: _____

Question 15: _____

Reason for difficulty: _____

Discuss

Verbally compare your decisions with those of the classmates in your discussion group. Explain and defend your opinions. Listen carefully to your classmates' opinions, but do not be afraid to disagree with those opinions. Try to reach a group consensus on the best solution to the problem. One person in the group should write down the group's decision.

Extend

1. Do you think that humans will ever be able to prove scientifically the existence of God? What effect would such a confirmation have on the world?

2. Why do you think that governments spend more money building weapons of destruction than researching cures for disease?

3. Explain to the class what exciting possibilities you see in your own job or field of study.

4. Moving from the physical universe to philosophy: What is beauty? Write a definition of what you think beauty is, and compare it with those of your classmates.

Glossary

Meanings are given as they refer to the context of the corresponding reading. The number in parentheses refers to the unit in which the word appears.

accessible (7): available. *Ex.* In a library, books are *accessible* to all people.

acclaimed (23): recognized. *Ex.* Pélé has been *acclaimed* as the best soccer player ever.

administrative manpower (1): managers. *Ex. Administrative manpower* is necessary for a government to function properly.

advances (19): accomplishments. *Ex.* Achieving nuclear peace and feeding the world's hungry will be major *advances*.

adversary (25): enemy. *Ex.* Although Mary is my *adversary*, she is your friend.

affirmative action (23): policy to give a certain percentage of positions to minority students. *Ex. Affirmative action* is necessary to correct the injustices of past discrimination.

aides (5): helpers. *Ex.* The President's *aides* were responsible for the scandal.

aimed toward (22): trying to get. *Ex.* He *aimed toward* a score of 660 on the TOEFL test.

allegedly (21): supposedly. *Ex.* The man *allegedly* stole the bicycle.

ally (25): friend. *Ex.* The socialist *allies* fought together against imperialism.

ambidextrous (3): capable of using both hands equally well. *Ex.* Good athletes must be *ambidextrous*.

ambiguity (20): vagueness. *Ex.* Most political speeches are full of *ambiguity*.

ample (20): enough. *Ex.* They have *ample* money to buy a Mercedes.

anonymous (6): without name. *Ex.* The newspaper won't publish *anonymous* letters.

appealing (4): likeable. *Ex.* Indonesians find spicy food *appealing*.

appeal to (22): attract. *Ex.* Flowers *appeal to* bees.

appointed (4): chosen. *Ex.* The committee was *appointed* by the chairperson.

approaching (11): coming nearer. *Ex.* We are *approaching* the year 2000.

are obliged to (14): must. *Ex.* Persons *are obliged to* question authority.

articles (16): things. *Ex.* Various *articles* of warm clothing are important for Antarctic travel.

artificial insemination/conception (3): the process of impregnating by medical means. *Ex.* The champion racehorse was conceived by *artificial insemination*.

aside from (27): in addition to. *Ex. Aside from* biology, Bill enjoys classical music.

assets (18): items of value. *Ex.* As a wife and mother, President Jones thinks that one of her main *assets* is her family.

bill of rights (20): specific list of what citizens can do. *Ex.* Countries with totalitarian governments usually have no *bill of rights*.

book editor (17): person who chooses what books to publish. *Ex. Book editors* must feel the pulse of the public.

boundaries (9): borders. *Ex.* The *boundaries* of one's imagination are infinite.

bout (2): battle. *Ex.* After her *bout* with depression, Mary decided to see a psychiatrist.

breakthroughs (23): advances. *Ex.* Computers have led to many technological *breakthroughs*.

brilliant (23): very intelligent. *Ex.* The Nobel Prize winner delivered a *brilliant* acceptance speech.

budget (1): financial plan. *Ex.* Although the country has a *budget* deficit, nobody seems concerned.

campaign (6): process of seeking political office. *Ex.* Rajiv Gandhi's political *campaign* emphasized the ideas of his mother.

cartoons (4): animated children's programs. *Ex.* Walt Disney created *cartoons* starring Mickey Mouse.

cast your ballot (6): vote. *Ex.* As a citizen in a democracy, you should *cast your ballot* in every election.

catchy (22): lively. *Ex.* "I'd like to buy the world a Coke" was a *catchy* slogan of the Coca-Cola Company.

characteristics (3): features (for example, height, weight). *Ex.* Black stripes and white stripes are *characteristics* of zebras.

charges (6): accusations. *Ex.* Murder was one of the *charges* against the criminal.

chief (27): leader. *Ex.* Geronimo, a famous *chief* of the Apache Indians, led many battles against the U.S. Army.

chorus (5): singing group: *Ex.* The *chorus* sang Verdi's *Aida.*

chronic (18): uncontrollable. *Ex. Chronic* back pain can be helped by exercise.

civilization (27): society and culture. *Ex.* Chinese *civilization* provided the world with paper and gunpowder.

civil suit (21): non-criminal legal action. *Ex.* The child's mother brought a *civil suit* against the toystore owner.

competent (13): capable. *Ex.* A foot doctor is not *competent* to perform a heart transplant.

compose (11): write. *Ex.* Beethoven *composed* nine symphonies.

compulsory (5): required. *Ex.* Elementary school attendance should be *compulsory* in all countries.

confirm (17): make sure of. *Ex.* The laboratory test may *confirm* the doctor's opinion that the patient has cancer.

core (13): basic. *Ex.* Do you think that mathematics is the *core* science?

cornerstone (26): part of building that contains time capsule. *Ex.* The old *cornerstone* was found when the building was destroyed.

counseling (12): advising. *Ex.* Juvenile drug users need consistent peer *counseling.*

creativity (9): imagination. *Ex.* Michelangelo's *creativity* in producing the sculpture of Moses is perhaps unparalleled.

critical deficiency (21): serious problem. *Ex.* Japan suffers from a *critical deficiency* of raw materials.

currents (16): fast-moving waters. *Ex.* Rafting in strong river *currents* is very dangerous.

curriculum (13): school courses. *Ex.* The university's *curriculum* needs to be expanded.

cut (5): reduced. *Ex.* In the new budget, military expenditures have been *cut.*

debate (5): verbal argument to decide the best answer to a question. *Ex.* The *debate* continues over whether to require military education in state-supported colleges.

decent (12): good. *Ex.* After having led a *decent* life, the lawyer turned to crime.

delegates to (28): members of. *Ex.* The *delegates to* the U.N. from Gabon voted in favor of the resolution.

delivery (15): birth. *Ex.* Unlike in the past, fathers today assist in the *delivery* of their children.

dense (1): heavy. *Ex.* Because of its *dense* population, Japan has little space for development.

depriving (15): taking something away from. *Ex. Depriving* a person of oxygen will soon cause their death.

designated (7): chosen. *Ex.* The new member was *designated* as a nominee for Treasurer.

detailed (9): very specific. *Ex.* Vesalius' *detailed* sketches of the human body led to the science of physiology.

deteriorate (2): become worse. *Ex.* Cement sidewalks *deteriorate* very slowly.

deteriorating (2): worsening. *Ex.* The *deteriorating* value of the dollar is hurting the U.S. economy.

devices (16): appliances. *Ex.* Microscopes are *devices* that enable one to see into another world.

disciplined (15): punished. *Ex.* The student was *disciplined* for inappropriate behavior.

discontent (4): unhappiness. *Ex.* Because of his *discontent* with his country's political system, the athlete immigrated to the U.S.

discretion (23): choice. *Ex.* Which nurses to hire will be left to the hospital supervisor's *discretion*.

disfiguring (21): changing the shape of. *Ex.* The operation *disfigured* the patient's stomach with large scars.

diverse (16): varied. *Ex.* The class is composed of *diverse* nationalities and personalities.

documentaries (4): news stories. *Ex.* The producer received an award for his *documentaries* on the war in Vietnam.

donate (2): give. *Ex.* John D. Rockefeller *donated* the land for the United Nations building in New York City.

donor heart (2): heart that will be put in a patient. *Ex.* A *donor heart* must be kept refrigerated until the transplant surgery begins.

dramatically (12): rapidly. *Ex.* The incidence of lung cancer in Singapore decreased *dramatically* when smoking was banned in public.

drastically (5): severely. *Ex.* Quantum mechanics *drastically* changed our conception of the universe.

drawing to a close (7): ending. *Ex.* As Shakespeare's *Othello* is *drawing to a close*, Othello kills his wife, Desdemona.

drive us (12): make us. *Ex.* The sound of dripping water can *drive us* crazy.

dropped in (12): came by. *Ex.* After Mary *dropped in* to visit me, she went shopping.

drought (18): lack of water. *Ex.* The Somalian *drought* has caused great suffering.

economic recession (18): bad economic period. *Ex.* Despite the *economic recession*, employment remained high.

electives (13): non-required courses chosen by a student. *Ex.* Geology and astronomy are *electives* offered at the university.

equivalent of (23): same as. *Ex.* Half a dozen eggs is the *equivalent of* six eggs.

eradicate (23): eliminate. *Ex.* Certain charities try to *eradicate* hunger in the world.

espionage (25): spying. *Ex.* James, Bond, Agent 007, fictitiously engaged in *espionage* for the United Kingdom.

excel (3): do extremely well. *Ex.* Thai dancers *excel* in the performance of their art.

extracurricular (5): outside the classroom. *Ex.* Soccer is an *extracurricular* activity at most American high schools.

feats (14): accomplishments. *Ex.* Hillary's and Norgay's conquest of Mt. Everest was one of history's major mountaineering *feats*.

federal support (7): government money. *Ex. Federal support* for family planning may be discontinued.

fire (5): throw out of a job. *Ex.* The manager was *fired* for changing the figures in his accounts.

flabby (7): fat. *Ex.* Lack of exercise makes a person *flabby*.

fleet (25): group. *Ex.* Aristotle Onassis had a large *fleet* of oil tankers.

from the rear (21): in the back. *Ex.* Twenty people were killed when the bus was hit *from the rear*.

funding (1): money. *Ex.* The scientist was unable to obtain *funding* for her project.

gain (5): receive. *Ex.* Abebe Akila *gained* fame as a long-distance runner from Ethiopia.

given a one-year suspended sentence (21): not required to go to prison. *Ex.* The judge refused to *give* the drunk driver *a one-year suspended sentence*.

good risks (18): people who will pay back loans. *Ex.* The bank will fail if it does not lend money to *good risks*.

governing council (20): group of leaders. *Ex.* The military government was replaced by a popularly elected *governing council*.

guidelines (9): laws. *Ex.* The government has issued new *guidelines* concerning visas.

harbor (25): protected water. *Ex.* The *harbor* in Sydney, Australia, is famous because the Sydney Opera House is located there.

hinder (1): block, slow down. *Ex.* Import taxes *hinder* free trade between nations.

image (18): public picture. *Ex.* As a result of his poor *image*, Jimmy Carter lost the 1980 U.S. presidential election.

impending (1): coming. *Ex.* The school closed because of the *impending* storm.

indigenous (1): native. *Ex.* The coffee plant is *indigenous* to Colombia.

informing (10): telling. *Ex.* Television can be an important means of *informing* the public about current problems.

initially (9): at first. *Ex. Initially*, Charles De Gaulle was a resistance fighter.

initiator (25): beginner. *Ex.* Black musicians in New Orleans were the *initiators* of American jazz.

innovative (9): imaginative. *Ex.* Even though the architect's ideas were *innovative*, they were rejected.

inquiries (28): questions. *Ex.* After the train accident, the government conducted *inquiries* into the health of the conductor.

inspiration (2): source of encouragement. *Ex.* Martin Luther King is an *inspiration* to people all over the world.

insure (11): guarantee. *Ex.* The volleyball team practiced to *insure* success.

intern (23): assistant doctor. *Ex.* Most *interns* work long hours and handle many cases.

intervention (25): action. *Ex.* The United Nations charter prohibits *intervention* by a country into the affairs of another.

in the heart of (9): in the center of. *Ex.* Atlanta is *in the heart of* the southern United States.

in the midst of (18): in the middle of. *Ex. In the midst of* great controversy, the Prime Minister resigned.

issue (11): publication. *Ex.* Next month, the first *issue* of the new magazine, *Sunrise*, will appear.

layout (9): plan. *Ex.* The *layout* of the condominium did not meet the city's building requirements.

left (10): given. *Ex.* The nephew hopes that he will be *left* a lot of money by his uncle.

long-lost (10): long-forgotten. *Ex.* The *long-lost* piece of jewelry was found in the back of the old dresser.

lottery (6): gambling game. *Ex.* The California *lottery* generates millions of dollars for public education.

lure (1): attract. *Ex.* Fishermen use different ways to *lure* fish to their hooks.

lush (16): abundant. *Ex.* Spring brings *lush* vegetation to the tropics.

maintain (18): keep and show. *Ex.* In an attempt to *maintain* order, the police used tear gas.

major (13): student's main field of interest. *Ex.* Bill's *major* is linguistics.

malnutrition (1): poor diet. *Ex.* The children in Detroit who had been suffering from *malnutrition* were saved by contributions of food.

manual (15): handbook of instructions. *Ex.* New cars come with an owner's *manual*.

manuscripts (17): unpublished books. *Ex.* The *manuscripts* were accepted for publication.

marketing campaign (22): selling plan. *Ex.* The company's *marketing campaign* for its new computer has been tremendously successful.

means of (16): way of. *Ex.* Intensive studying is a *means of* improving one's mind.

merely (17): only. *Ex.* Out of 100 invited guests, *merely* five people came to the meeting.

metropolitan (11): large-city. *Ex. Metropolitan* transportation often includes a subway system.

misconception (12): wrong idea. *Ex.* High school students often have a *misconception* about the difficulty of university study.

neurological (23): having to do with the nervous system. *Ex.* Toxic chemicals can cause *neurological* damage.

nominate (11): suggest. *Ex.* The popular president was *nominated* for a second term of office.

nurse (15): breast-feed. *Ex.* In some Middle Eastern cultures, babies are *nursed* until they are four years old.

nursing home (12): care facility for old, sick people. *Ex.* Incapable of looking after herself, the old woman was placed in a *nursing home*.

nutritious (5): healthful. *Ex.* A *nutritious* diet is essential for good health.

objectivity (11): fairness. *Ex.* Lacking *objectivity*, the judge removed herself from the trial.

obsolete (18): no longer used. *Ex.* Nothing becomes *obsolete* faster than military weapons.

organs (2): body parts such as eyes, heart. *Ex.* Alcohol damages many *organs*, including the liver and heart.

outstanding loans (18): loans that have not yet been paid. *Ex.* They have *outstanding loans* on their car and house.

parties (21): defendants. *Ex.* There were many *parties* involved in the suit concerning the airplane crash.

passive (3): not active, but acted upon. *Ex.* Mahatma Gandhi encouraged a philosophy of *passive* resistance.

patron (21): customer. *Ex.* A regular *patron* of the cafe, Mary especially loved the coffee.

policy (5): plan. *Ex.* Beverly Hills has a *policy* of no smoking in restaurants.

preliminary (17):   before the final decision. *Ex. Preliminary* studies reveal that aspirin may prevent heart disease.

premises (21): area. *Ex.* He is so anti-social that he has a sign on his gate that reads: ''Stay off the *premises!*''

press (20): newspapers, TV, radio, magazines. *Ex.* Freedom of the *press* is necessary for any democracy.

pressing (12): urgent. *Ex.* Finding places to store nuclear waste is one of the world's most *pressing* problems.

principles (20): ideas. *Ex.* Some *principles* of English grammar are difficult to understand.

projects (9): job. *Ex.* The *projects* included supplying water to the village.

property taxes (5): taxes on land, buildings. *Ex.* Because of high *property taxes*, low-income families cannot afford to buy houses.

prospective (15): expected. *Ex. Prospective* buyers of used cars should check the cars' engines very carefully.

prototypes (18): models. *Ex.* The Model T was one of the early *prototypes* of mass automobile production.

radically (3): completely. *Ex.* The discovery of DNA by scientists Watson and Crick *radically* changed the way we think of molecular structure.

rationale for (9): reasons behind. *Ex.* The psychiatrist attempted to discover the *rationale for* the woman's unusual behavior.

real estate agent (3): seller of land and houses. *Ex.* If you want to sell your house quickly, find a good *real estate agent*.

realistic (3): practical. *Ex.* No member could offer a *realistic* way for the club to get $100,000.

recipient (2): receiver. *Ex.* Anwar Sadat and Menachem Begin were each a 1977 *recipient* of the Nobel Peace Prize.

relatively (5): comparatively. *Ex.* Kauai is *relatively* less developed than the other Hawaiian Islands.

remainder (16): rest. *Ex.* After Susan finished studying chemistry, she spent the *remainder* of her evening relaxing.

renowned (2): famous. *Ex.* The actress is *renowned* for her beauty.

represents (9): stands for. *Ex.* On a road map, the ''tent'' symbol *represents* public campgrounds.

revealed (21): showed. *Ex.* An analysis of the situation *revealed* many problems.

R.N. (18): Registered Nurse. *Ex.* The patient is so sick that he needs an *R.N.* to spend the night in his room.

ruined (27): spoiled. *Ex.* Nearly *ruined* by 500 years of neglect, the Andean city of Macchu Picchu is being restored.

rupture (21): break open. *Ex. Rupture* a pipe and it is sure to leak.

"rush" (22): must be finished fast. *Ex.* The manager needs a *"rush"* job on this report.

scattered (1): spread. *Ex. Scattered* throughout the country, the new immigrants have blended into society.

seize (25): forcibly take. *Ex.* The rebels will *seize* the radio station.

seized (25): taken control of. *Ex.* The radio station has been *seized*.

sentenced (16): punished by a court. *Ex.* The burglar was *sentenced* to one year in prison.

settlers (20): first people to live in a place. *Ex.* Early European *settlers* in the American east found native peoples who had lived there for thousands of years.

shoplifting (12): stealing from a store. *Ex.* While the clerk was talking to one customer about a shirt, another person was *shoplifting* some underwear.

sixth sense (17): special idea. *Ex.* Mary has a *sixth sense* about people that helps her to understand them.

slogan (22): short phrase. *Ex.* In his novel *1984*, George Orwell predicted that governments would use crazy *slogans* such as "War is Peace" to control their citizens.

sobriety test (21): test for drunkenness. *Ex.* The policeman administered a *sobriety test* to drivers who had been stopped for speeding.

Social Security (12): retirement money. *Ex.* Many older people need *social security* to survive.

spear (27): hunting weapon. *Ex.* The tribesman killed the lion with a *spear*.

spots (23): positions. *Ex.* No new *spots* are opening in the company this year because of poor sales last year.

State of the Union message (26): Annual speech to the U.S. Congress about the country. *Ex.* The President's *State of the Union message* contained many references to domestic programs.

stipulation (10): restriction. *Ex.* The apartment lease contained one *stipulation*: "No pets allowed."

submitted (17): turned in. *Ex.* The research paper was *submitted* late and was poorly written.

suspending time (8): making the past and present the same time. *Ex.* Many novelists have written about the possibilities of *suspending time*.

systematically (28): in an organized way. *Ex.* Copernicus *systematically* considered all aspects of his theory before publishing it.

task (9): objective. *Ex.* Her *task* is to rid the country of disease.

team (2): group. *Ex.* Which *team* do you think will win the championship?

temperate (20): moderate. *Ex. Temperate* in habits, Peter leads a well-disciplined life.

time capsule (26): container with historical items in it. *Ex.* Historians can learn much through the analysis of *time capsules*.

tranquilizers (26): pills that help one relax. *Ex.* She becomes so nervous on airplanes that she must take *tranquilizers*.

treacherous (21): very dangerous. *Ex.* The bus ride down the mountain was *treacherous*.

tributaries (1): small rivers carrying water to a large river. *Ex.* When its *tributaries* dried up, the volume of water in the Nile decreased dramatically.

tried (25): taken to court. *Ex. Tried* and convicted of treason, the soldier was shot.

troops (25): soldiers *Ex.* Invading *troops* took over the country.

trustees (13): directors. *Ex.* The corporation's board of *trustees* elected a new chairperson.

tumors (23): cancers. *Ex.* Some *tumors* cannot yet be successfully treated.

ultimate job (2): job after graduation. *Ex.* Having majored in physical education, Jack's *ultimate job* will be that of a physical education instructor.

under the influence (21): drunk. *Ex.* The teenager was arrested for being *under the influence*.

variation (3): flexibility. *Ex.* There is little temperature *variation* in Tahiti.

verify (21): check. *Ex.* We could not *verify* the report from the remote country.

veterans (6): former soldiers. *Ex.* All *veterans* receive special benefits from the government.

violate (25): trespass. *Ex.* The plane was shot down for *violating* the country's air space.

warrior (27): person responsible for protecting or fighting. *Ex.* For being an excellent *warrior*, the young woman was rewarded with a horse.

welfare (2): government money for poor people. *Ex.* As the economy declined, the number of people on *welfare* increased.

will (10): legal paper with dead person's wishes. *Ex.* His *will* left all his money to charities.